CHARLES E. WILSON
*and Controversy at the Pentagon,
1953 to 1957*

Charles E. Wilson, secretary of defense.

By permission of the Wilson Archives

Charles E. Wilson

and Controversy at the Pentagon, 1953 to 1957

E. BRUCE GEELHOED
BALL STATE UNIVERSITY

WAYNE STATE UNIVERSITY PRESS
DETROIT, 1979

Library of Congress Cataloging in Publication Data

Geelhoed, E. Bruce, 1948–
 Charles E. Wilson and controversy at the Pentagon,
1953 to 1957.

 Bibliography: p.
 Includes index.
 1. United States. Dept. of Defense—History.
2. Wilson, Charles Erwin, 1890–1961. 3. United States—
Politics and government—1953–1961. I. Title.
UA23.6.G43   353.6′092′4 [B]   79-9756
ISBN 0-8143-1635-2

Contents

Illustrations 7

Acknowledgments 9

1 Introduction 13

2 "A Cemetery for Dead Cats":
Wilson's Introduction to the Defense Department 21

3 The Furor over Confirmation 40

4 New Problems, Personalities, and Policies:
Wilson and the Defense Department in 1953 59

5 Combating Hysteria: The Internal Security Issue 82

6 Wilson and the New Look 100

7 The Opposition in Revolt: Army-Air Power Controversies 121

8 Draft-dodgers and Dunghills:
Controversy over the National Guard 149

9 "Efficiency Experts Have Never Been Popular":
Wilson's Administration of the Defense Department 164

10 Wilson in Perspective 178

Notes 183

Bibliography 204

Index 211

Illustrations

Charles E. Wilson, secretary of defense. frontispiece

Secretary of Defense Robert A. Lovett and
Secretary-designate Wilson at a press conference. 25

Secretaries-designate of the national military
establishment. 25

Secretary-designate Wilson, President-elect Eisenhower,
and military leaders in South Korea. 35

"It's Not Customary, Mr. Wilson" 43

One Way to Help Balance the Budget 44

New Top Man on the Pentagon Totem Pole 53

Wilson at his swearing-in as secretary of defense. 55

There's No Such Thing as a Perfect Defense 75

Cartoon from the *Washington Evening Star,*
4 September 1953. 77

Admiral Arthur Radford
and Secretary of Defense Wilson. 79

Secretary of Defense Wilson visiting the
U.S. Air Force base in Frankfurt, Germany. 79

Secretary of State Dulles, President Eisenhower, and
Secretary of Defense Wilson at a televised cabinet meeting. 103

We May Have to Take Another 'New Look'! 109

"George, Let Me Show You Something"   111

Secretary of Defense Wilson with a
group of cartoonists.   113

With Regards to "Ike's Master of Hounds"   113

The Eisenhower cabinet, 29 July 1955.   116

Secretary of Defense Wilson before a
Senate subcommittee.   123

"Not in the Corridors, Dammit!"   127

"Amazing"   129

'Massive Retaliation'   135

"Ezra, You Got Any Storage Bins You're Not Using?"   145

"I Can Do It for You Wholesale"   147

"The Trouble with You, Charlie, Is That
You Say What You Think"   153

King of the Hill   155

'And I Was Beginning to Feel Sorry for Mr. Dulles!'   159

"Leave Something for Me, Charlie"   169

Secretary of Defense Wilson at a
defense production facility.   171

Secretary of Defense Wilson and military leaders
in South Korea.   171

Acknowledgments

T<small>HIS</small> book is dedicated to my family: my wife Deborah, my parents, Mr. and Mrs. Edward Geelhoed, and my son, Marc Edward. I am indebted to them for their support and encouragement in the writing of this work.

I also wish to thank a number of helpful people who have assisted me in completing this study. Larry Osnes, the archivist of the Charles E. Wilson Archives, and Lynn Goldman, his assistant, answered a multitude of questions about Wilson's papers. C. Warren Vander Hill and Dwight W. Hoover, two colleagues at Ball State University, provided encouragement and constructive criticism in directing the writing of this book in its early stages as a doctoral dissertation. Alacia Green expertly typed the various drafts of the manuscript.

The Honorable Thomas S. Gates, John A. Hannah, H. Struve Hensel, Wilfred J. McNeil, and Carey A. Randall, five of Charles Wilson's associates at the Defense Department, graciously responded to my questions about Wilson's administration of the Pentagon and deserve my gratitude. William MacKinnon and Marel Anne Thomas of General Motors Corporation supplied useful information about Wilson's years as the president of General Motors.

Sherwyn T. Carr, a considerate and candid editor, was immensely helpful in preparing the manuscript for press. Mike Thielen and Karen Fortier assisted in some final technical details. All errors are mine.

CHARLES E. WILSON
and Controversy at the Pentagon,
1953 to 1957

1

Introduction

C HARLES E. Wilson served as secretary of defense from 1953 to 1957, a period which included all of President Dwight D. Eisenhower's first term and almost one year of his second. Through his tenure at the Pentagon, Wilson became known as one of Washington's most colorful and controversial figures. An individual of immense personal wealth, which he had earned in private industry as a General Motors executive, Wilson was nonetheless a man of simple tastes and habits. He scorned affectation and was a tireless worker, often devoting seventy-two-hour work weeks to his responsibilities at the Defense Department. Not entirely comfortable around politicians and the Washington press corps, Wilson nevertheless had won the affection of Capitol reporters and the respect, if not the admiration, of his critics by the time he retired from government service in October 1957.

In the past several years, journalists and historians have begun to examine the Eisenhower presidency in detail. Certainly the general's eight-year administration, as well as the personalities who shaped power under him, constitute fertile grounds for research. Previous discussions of Wilson's role in the Eisenhower administration have centered chiefly on the secretary's personality and administrative style, rather than on the strengths and weaknesses of his managerial performance at the Pentagon. Of course, separating an individual's personal characteristics from the conduct of his work has never been a simple task. Indeed, it is especially difficult when considering "Engine Charlie" Wilson, who made little effort to conceal his feelings and often found himself in the Washington spotlight.

At any rate, much of the literature now existing on the Eisenhower administration does not contain positive interpretations of Wilson. In the late 1950s and early 1960s, journalists such as Robert Donovan, Marquis Childs, and Emmett John Hughes submitted the first commentaries on the Eisenhower years. During the 1970s, Herbert S. Parmet, Townsend Hoopes, Charles C. Alexander, and Douglas Kinnard contributed worthwhile studies of the general's presidency. Although historians and journalists have differed on some points regarding the administration, they seem to agree that Wilson's career in business, as well as his tendency to let slip inappropriate political comments, caused him great difficulty in performing his duties.[1] According to this view, Wilson was ill equipped to handle complex problems of public policy because his corporate experience precluded a flexible approach to political questions. As a production specialist while the president of General Motors, Wilson was unexcelled, but as a cabinet member, he was either too "narrowly provincial" or "unphilosophic" to perform successfully. Some have argued that Wilson failed to make the transition from the orderly corporate bureaucracy to the less comprehensible federal bureaucracy.[2] Furthermore, some writers have seen Wilson's occasional embarrassing statements as proof that the secretary failed to understand the realities of political life in Washington.[3]

To the extent that Wilson was often a controversial figure in Washington, one could assume that the prevailing interpretation of his shortcomings is correct. Yet the secretary was popular with a sizable percentage of the American people while he served under Eisenhower. Many citizens considered Wilson's previous experience in private industry to be an asset, not a liability, for one in public service. Even after the negative publicity which he received as a result of his well-known "what's good for General Motors" testimony before the Senate Armed Services Committee, Wilson found that much of the public applauded his performance. Furthermore, Wilson's personal behavior contrasted sharply with that of other administration officials. While Secretary of State John Foster Dulles, for example, presented a cold, serious, and taciturn image to the public, Wilson was warm, outgoing, and quotable. In the words of Marquis Childs, Wilson "was a likable person. He was what he was and no nonsense about it." During his stay in Washington, the secretary received thousands of admiring letters from Americans who felt a personal identification with him.[4]

One Washington observer compared Wilson's behavior to that of another plainspoken midwesterner, Harry S. Truman.[5] Wilson's hierarchy of personal values, like Truman's, emphasized loyalty, common sense, and the individual's obligation to stand up for his beliefs and hold to them until proven wrong. Thus, Wilson proved to be a determined administrator who was unswervingly devoted to Eisenhower. But in addition, he possessed enough political courage to insist that Pentagon expenditures be kept down in spite of pressure from Congress and the military to raise defense spending. When official Washington trembled at the anti-Communist witch-hunt of Senator Joseph McCarthy, the secretary not only refused to appear before McCarthy's committee, but he also labeled the senator's charges against government officials "damn tommyrot."[6]

A study of Wilson as a central, rather than a peripheral, figure in the administration not only reveals much about Wilson's performance as secretary of defense, but also about the manner in which Eisenhower conducted his presidency. Certainly, national defense policy and Wilson's administration of it were explosive, partisan issues during the 1950s. By itself, national defense policy is a complex matter, containing elements of domestic politics, foreign affairs, and the national economy. The secretary of defense needed a knowledge of and sensitivity to all these elements in order to present a rational defense policy before the Congress and the American people. Before Wilson could make such a presentation, however, he was required to understand the goals established by Eisenhower for his administration.

In retrospect, it appears that one of Eisenhower's major objectives as president was to bring about a stable national economy. Eisenhower, perhaps conditioned by what Daniel Boorstin has termed a "Cincinnatus complex," wanted to turn federal policy in the direction of a civilian-oriented economy.[7] Haunted by the experiences of two recent wars, both Eisenhower and the American people longed for peace accompanied by economic prosperity and domestic serenity. As a result, administration leaders saw balanced federal budgets, reductions in personal and corporate income taxes, and minimal governmental interference in the free enterprise system as the best means of attaining prosperity without inflation. Eisenhower, Wilson, Secretary of the Treasury George M. Humphrey, and the president's economic advisers spoke as one in their view that massive federal deficits could eventually bankrupt the nation and regiment civilian life. The policy of fiscal restraint, however, conflicted in some ways with the administration's anti-Communist foreign policy. As expressed by Secretary of State Dulles, that policy seemed to commit the United States to a never-ending Cold War with the Communist bloc. Taken to its extreme, it meant higher defense budgets, increased taxes, and greater federal deficits.

The administration therefore was compelled to make a fundamental decision from its outset: would it insist on reduced defense costs to accommodate its domestic economic policy or would it increase military spending to reassure those who feared a military conflict with the Soviet Union? Eisenhower and Humphrey decided to instruct Wilson that expenditures for defense needed to be scaled down, while at the same time permitting Dulles to continue the hard-line rhetoric of the Cold War.[8]

Because Eisenhower and Humphrey agreed on a policy of fiscal restraint, Wilson administered a defense program fundamentally different from that of the Truman administration. Truman's defense policy adhered to the recommendations contained in a National Security Council memorandum, NSC-68, adopted in 1950. The representatives from the State Department and the military establishment who wrote NSC-68 argued that the indefinite nature of the Cold War could require the United States to spend up to 20 percent of its gross national product in order to maintain military superiority over the Soviet Union. Such a military buildup, the planners reasoned, would allow the United States to resist Communist aggression anywhere in the world. NSC-68 became the military backbone of the so-called containment policy, and Truman stepped toward a tacit acknowledgment that the United States would be the world's policeman. Military spending skyrocketed during Truman's administration, a result of both the outbreak of the Korean War and the cost of trying to meet the recommendations of NSC-68.[9]

Eisenhower and Wilson adopted a different outlook on defense, tending to follow the philosophy of the containment policy while rejecting its cost. Eisenhower did not believe the United States could afford to spend 20 percent of its gross national product on defense, fearing that such expenditures could bankrupt the country in the long run. Indeed, he said during the 1952 campaign: "We must achieve both security and solvency. In fact, the foundation of military strength is economic strength. A bankrupt America is more the Soviet goal than an America conquered on the field of battle."[10] Eisenhower's warnings against large-scale defense spending were not simply rhetoric designed to appeal to cost-conscious voters. The president continued his resistance to the financial demands of the military throughout his two terms in office, even during periods of crisis. As he told a group of advisers in 1958: "I determined that this [Berlin] crisis should not affect our long-range plans for assuring the defense of America without waste. Indeed, it was always my conviction that one purpose of Khrushchev's manufactured crisis was to frighten free populations and governments into unnecessary and debilitating spending sprees."[11]

Wilson was later to echo the president's thoughts as to what America could, and could not, afford for defense. Indeed, he helped to redirect the national defense policy from the Truman administration's stated goal of strategic superiority over the Soviet Union to one of relative American sufficiency vis-à-vis Russian military power. He wrote in a 1956 article for *Nation's Business*: "Military expenditures must be adequate, but not so great that they will become an intolerable burden which will harm the social and economic fabric of our country. True security cannot be founded on arms and arms alone."[12]

While Eisenhower and Wilson shared the Truman administration's view that Cold War tensions promised to remain indefinitely, they were skeptical of the idea that a massive military buildup was the best method of coping with the Communist threat. Nor did they believe that the United States possessed the long-range capability to act as the world's policeman. When French troops were besieged by the Viet Minh at Dienbienphu in Vietnam during the spring of 1954, pressure for some kind of direct American aid to the French built within the Congress and the military. But Eisenhower refrained from intervening because he lacked support from American allies and also because the United Nations was reluctant to become involved in the Vietnamese situation. During that same spring, Wilson expressed his views on the matter of American intervention. Noting that many of America's allies had colonial interests, Wilson stated that any American intervention into colonial struggles could be perceived by "our allies as an attempt to dominate their business." It was also possible that interfering in conflicts among developing nations could damage America's future relations with them. "Even good policemen aren't popular very long," Wilson concluded.[13]

Because the Eisenhower administration substituted sufficiency for strategic superiority as a goal of American defense policy, Wilson adopted the philosophy that American arms served a primarily defensive purpose. He outlined that idea in 1956, when he wrote that "military forces in America are maintained to defend a way of life, not for aggression."[14] Because Dulles often chose such words as "brinkmanship," "liberation," "roll-back," and "massive retaliation" to describe the potential uses of American power, some confusion existed during the 1950s as to whether the United States intended to use its military strength offensively or defensively. Admittedly, there were striking advances in nuclear technology and the development of terrifying new weapons systems while Wilson was secretary of defense. Yet Wilson's speeches, testimony to congressional committees, and press conferences show that the secretary held to a fundamentally defensive conception of the use of American power.[15] As a spokesman for national defense, Wilson was not a hard-liner, and his behavior lends support to those who contend that the administration was genuinely interested in reducing East-West tensions.[16]

While Wilson was often a controversial political personality and the administration's defense policy became a partisan issue, so also did Wilson's administrative performance occasion much debate in Washington during the 1950s. An understanding of Wilson's approach to Pentagon administration is an aid in evaluating his importance to the administration and also in showing how Eisenhower's methods differed from those of his predecessors.

Two principles seem to apply regarding the Eisenhower-Wilson relationship. First, Eisenhower was his own secretary of defense where broad outlines of military policy were involved, which is hardly surprising given his military background.[17] Eisenhower's military experience served the administration (and Wilson specifically) well by helping to win public support for its defense policy. Challenging Eisenhower's military logic, and then winning public acceptance for that challenge, proved to be a political task beyond the reach of most congressmen and senators during the 1950s. Second, while the president developed the defense philosophy, he delegated a great deal of authority to Wilson in administering and managing details. Consequently, Wilson possessed a wide range of managerial responsibilities which gave him considerable political power even though the president retained ultimate authority.

When Wilson first began work at the Defense Department, he apparently was uncomfortable with the degree of independence Eisenhower granted him. For a time, he requested weekly meetings with Eisenhower in order to discuss Pentagon business. Eisenhower, however, wanted bureaucratic problems ironed out by cabinet members. Finally he told Wilson: "Charlie, you run defense. We both can't do it, and I won't do it. I was elected to worry about a lot of other things than the day-to-day operations of a department."[18] Eisenhower's instruction to Wilson that he "run" his department was significant; Wilson's primary responsibility in the administration was a managerial one. Because Eisenhower and Humphrey had taken the lead on developing policy, Wilson became a spokesman and management specialist for the administration on the one specific issue of national defense. In that role, however, Wilson played an important part in the implementation of the administration's defense policy, and it is one which should not be overlooked. Wilson's role in the administration, in other words, was not primarily political, although it did require a certain amount of what might be labeled political skill. Consequently, Eisenhower never forced Wilson's resignation when the secretary was under attack from congressmen, senators, military leaders, and the press because of a particular unpopular decision.

Wilson presided over a significant programmatic shift in defense operations between 1953 and 1957. He reduced the size of the standing army, encouraged the development of newer and more modern weapons systems, gave a special emphasis to upgrading nuclear technology, and instituted a cost-conscious approach to Pentagon management. These policies often brought criticism from legislators and military leaders who charged that Wilson intended to "wreck" this or that particular program. But Eisenhower had warned Wilson that he "had to be willing to be the most unpopular man in government," and he supported the secretary of defense through the political storms.[19] Even when his blunt statements created some embarrassment for the administration, Wilson remained in the cabinet because the president apparently remained satisfied that the secretary was "running" the Defense Department acceptably.

"The price of progress is trouble," Wilson told a news conference in May 1956.[20] By that statement, he accurately described his tenure as secretary of defense. During his term in office, Wilson encountered more than his share of trouble, but he also managed the Pentagon for four-and-a-half years, almost three times longer than any of his predecessors. Understanding Wilson's administrative performance, as well as his lively and controversial political style, provides a significant insight into the Eisenhower years.

2

"A Cemetery For Dead Cats":
Wilson's Introduction to the Defense Department

ALTHOUGH Charles E. Wilson had directed a massive industrial organization at General Motors, he may well have been surprised at the enormous administrative task which the Department of Defense represented in 1953. Created by the National Security Act of 1947 (later amended in 1949), it had become the largest agency in government as well as the world's biggest employer and purchaser. As Wilson later told the Senate Armed Services Committee, he was "risking failure" by accepting Dwight D. Eisenhower's request to serve as secretary of defense.[1] During its stormy history between 1947 and 1952, the department had been involved in military matters ranging from the development of nuclear weapons to the interservice feuding which seriously threatened morale in the armed forces. The arming of the nation's allies in Europe and the supervision of a shooting war in Korea further complicated the department's tasks. Added to these military and strategic matters was the complex and frustrating responsibility of administration. Problems of procurement, production, storage, transportation, and personnel required the defense secretary's attention. The combined pressures resulting from these strategic, planning, and management responsibilities created such bureaucratic havoc for the administration of President Harry S. Truman that James V. Forrestal, the first secretary of defense, once lamented that his office would become "the greatest cemetery for dead cats in history."[2]

When one remembers that the Defense Department was a new bureaucratic institution given tremendous responsibilities, its early history of conflict and confusion comes as no surprise. Faced with a disorganized military policy and a headlong demobilization immediately after World War II, President Truman had seen that the realities of the Cold War required the development of a comprehensive national defense program. A veteran of World War I as well as a former senator who had investigated the production effort during World War II, Truman was familiar with the planning, logistic, and personnel problems involved in maintaining a sound military program. However, developments in nuclear technology, combined with America's postwar commitments as a leader of the free world, increased the nation's defense burden beyond anything envisioned prior to World War II. Wishing to consolidate national defense functions, Congress, on Truman's initiative, enacted the National Security Act, which authorized the creation of a National Military Establishment headed by a civilian secretary of defense. The legislation also created the National Security Council, the Central Intelligence Agency, and the National Security Resources Board.[3] The secretary of defense was to serve as overall coordinator of defense policy and as the focus of civilian and military advice for the formulation of national security decisions. The various armed service secretaries and uniformed military leaders, however, remained free to consult with the president on policy matters.

In securing this legislation, Truman hoped to strengthen civilian control over the military, to unify (to the extent possible) the planning, strategic, and operations functions of the armed services, and to coordinate military activity with economic and foreign policy. These goals certainly represented a worthy effort on Truman's part to bring order to an emerging military establishment. Problems soon developed, however. Forrestal discovered that the secretary of defense lacked sufficient authority to carry out the administration's objectives. This realization carried with it a measure of embarrassment, as Forrestal had previously argued that no single individual should be given broad managerial powers over the Pentagon.[4] Throughout his tenure as secretary of defense, Forrestal searched diligently for the administrative balance which would provide the defense secretary with the measure of authority necessary to exert leadership over his department without his becoming, in effect, the czar of military production, personnel, and operations.

Truman's relatively stringent economic policies also affected the development of the department. At no time prior to the Korean War did the president favor a defense appropriation greater than $14.4 billion.[5] The scarcity of funds for military spending resulted in intense interservice competition for the available money. Samuel P. Huntington described this scramble for dollars, especially between the Navy and Air Force, as "a permanent fixture of the military scene between 1947–1949."[6] Forrestal found himself under constant bureaucratic pressure, either from the military with its demands for preparedness or from Truman and his budgeteers with their emphasis on economy.

A supremely dedicated individual, Forrestal tolerated a bad situation which continually threatened to become worse. By 1949, however, he had prepared a set of recommendations which would help in securing his defense objectives. These proposals strengthened the authority of the secretary of defense, provided personnel assistance to the secretary in managing the Pentagon, and specified a more advisory role for the military in the determination of national security policy. According to the National Security Act Amendments of 1949, the Department of Defense came into existence as a new cabinet-level department. The Army, Navy, and Air Force became military departments within this new department, which was commonly referred to as "the Pentagon" because of its location in the sprawling new complex of offices constructed for the old War Department during World War II. The secretary of defense received three civilian assistant secretaries to assist him in the areas of finance, international security, and manpower. The civilian administrators of the armed service branches and the military leadership reported directly to the secretary of defense.[7] This significant reform of policies and procedures came not a whit too soon. By the end of 1950, the United States would be called upon to carry out the rearming of Western Europe, decide the fate of research and development for the hydrogen bomb, and fight a so-called police action in Korea. The Pentagon played critical roles in each of these events, and the secretary of defense's importance in the government increased dramatically.

During his presidency, Truman employed four different defense secretaries. Forrestal, the first secretary of defense, served from September 1947 to March 1949 and pioneered in the development of the office's functions. Louis Johnson followed Forrestal and held the office until the Korean conflict became a crisis in September 1950. George C. Marshall, army chief of staff during World War II and secretary of state during the early Truman years, replaced Johnson and served for one year until he relinquished the post to his able deputy, Robert A. Lovett. Lovett administered the Defense Department until the conclusion of Truman's presidency in January 1953.[8]

None of Truman's defense secretaries ever really mastered the details of the office, although it must be said that each man made conscientious efforts to solve the problems of the military establishment. In the parlance of some defense analysts, Forrestal and Lovett took a "generalist" approach to the administration of the Pentagon and therefore became involved in the whole range of strategic decision making and policy formulation. Johnson, on the other hand, represented a more "functionalist" approach, serving as the administrator of a national security policy determined by Truman and other administration officials. Marshall's role fit neither description, although he certainly adopted a more generalist than functionalist approach to his position. Appointed by Truman to manage the Korean War effort and correct serious deficiencies in mobilization, Marshall did not have to face some of the administrative problems which vexed his predecessors. As the individual most responsible for organizing the military effort during World War II, Marshall had earned a military reputation unparalleled within the councils of government. This reputation, combined with the respect he had won as Truman's secretary of state, strengthened his position at the Pentagon when he became defense secretary.[9] But like Truman's other defense secretaries, Marshall found the position a strain, physically, mentally, and emotionally. By analyzing the difficulties which Truman's four secretaries encountered, it is possible to determine how the office developed to the point where Wilson found it in 1952 and also why Eisenhower selected him for the position on the basis of his past experience.

Forrestal, Johnson, Marshall, and Lovett faced problems in four interrelated areas: maintaining the confidence of the president and of other cabinet officials that defense policy was well coordinated with economic and foreign policy; retaining the support of the military on matters related to strategy and to each service's mission and roles;

Secretary of Defense Robert A. Lovett and Secretary-designate Wilson at a press conference on 26 November 1952.

Secretaries-designate of the national military establishment at a Pentagon meeting on 23 December 1952. Front, left to right: Wilson; Roger M. Kyes (deputy secretary, Defense). Back, left to right: Robert T. Stevens (Army); Robert B. Anderson (Navy); Harold B. Talbott (Air Force).

managing the sprawling operations of the Defense Department; and, finally, keeping abreast of rapidly changing technology, including developments in nuclear weaponry. The common thread running through each of these problem areas was the defense budget and disagreements within the administration over its appropriate size. As Forrestal and Johnson discovered (and Marshall and Lovett found to a lesser degree), it was virtually impossible for the defense secretary to strike an adequate balance between the administration's overall economic policy objectives and the military's stated security requirements.

Truman's initial choice for the first secretary of defense was Secretary of War Robert Patterson, who refused the position to return to civilian life. Forrestal, after his appointment in 1947, strongly influenced the direction of the Pentagon's policies and procedures. The son of an Irish immigrant, Forrestal was a man of tremendous energy and force. He entered the government during World War II after building a prosperous business career as an investment banker in New York, serving as secretary of the navy under President Franklin Roosevelt. Administratively competent and a serious student of the civilian military establishment, Forrestal became especially important after the war, when the Truman administration began formulating plans for consolidation of the military establishment. The Army and the Navy differed, of course, in their ideas for the unification of the armed services. The Army favored an organization similar to the one used during World War II, when General Marshall served as chief of staff and, in that role, was the president's principal military adviser. As secretary of the navy, Forrestal led the fight for a more civilian-oriented program, and his views ultimately prevailed.

As well qualified for the post as any man, Forrestal immediately ran into trouble in the position. Hamstrung by the failure of the National Security Act of 1947 to provide the defense secretary with adequate staff support, Forrestal was unable effectively to coordinate the diverse Pentagon operations. Furthermore, the armed service secretaries still possessed authority to state their independent cases to the president. Truman also had insisted that the military leaders have a similar prerogative, another action which undercut the authority of the defense secretary. Truman's rigorous enforcement of stringent budgetary guidelines for the federal government in 1947 and 1948 created additional problems for Forrestal within the department. Forrestal did not differ with the president's economic conservatism, but he nevertheless found it difficult to satisfy the fiscal demands of the armed services. To meet the situation, he advocated a "balanced forces" approach, by which each service would have responsibilities in the conventional and strategic areas, but the defense secretary would make decisions regarding the total cost of the national defense program. At a conference in Key West, Florida, in March 1948, Forrestal managed to gain the agreement of the service secretaries and the military leadership on a roles-and-missions statement which placed national defense policy within Truman's budgetary philosophy.[10]

Forrestal's problems intensified throughout 1948, despite the apparent understandings reached at Key West. Not only did disagreements between the Army, Navy, and Air Force continue to flare up, but Forrestal soon found himself at odds with the president. In late June 1948, the Soviets closed American access to Berlin. The Russian action, taken at the time of the Republican national convention, represented a clear challenge by the Soviets to Truman's leadership during a presidential election year. Insisting that the American presence in West Berlin was validated by agreement, Truman intended the nation to maintain it, and he soon ordered an airlift to supply the residents of the beleaguered city.[11] Within the administration's councils, Forrestal vacillated in his support of the airlift. The secretary of defense began to lose the confidence of the president, the one "absolutely essential weapon" he needed for effectiveness in office.[12]

As events progressed in 1948, Forrestal continued to lose stature within the administration. He differed with Truman on the direction of nuclear weapons policy, arguing that the Air Force should have a voice in the decision making on the use of the atomic bomb. Truman insisted that those decisions remain in the Oval Office.[13] Forrestal asserted that he could not reduce the next defense budget below $16.9 billion; Truman insisted that $14.4 billion be the Pentagon's maximum appropriation. Although he refrained from any personal campaigning in Truman's reelection bid, Forrestal briefed Thomas Dewey, the Republican nominee, on defense matters prior to the election. To Truman, who was fighting the political battle of his life,

Forrestal's action bordered on insubordination. Forrestal had also taken some positions on the Palestine issue which angered Jewish voters.[14] Although formulating the administration's policy on the Middle East seemed to be the responsibility of the State Department, Forrestal believed that "foreign policy is a function of defense and vice versa,"[15] and justified his support for an even-handed stance in the Middle East on the basis of the vast oil reserves in the Arab nations. By early 1949, however, it was clear that his views were unpopular in the administration. In March, Forrestal submitted his resignation to the president.

According to Truman's daughter Margaret, Forrestal "literally wore himself out in the service of his country." Conscientious perhaps to a fault, he had devoted exhausting hours for two years to placing the nation's defenses in a state of prepared readiness. Criticized on virtually every front, Forrestal eventually collapsed under the pressure and fell into prolonged depressions. In spite of the personal attacks on his performance, he left behind a record of substantial achievement. He had directed the Defense Department toward better fiscal procedures, established internal task forces to improve its efficiency, ordered that groups be organized to study weapons development, and demonstrated to the military that their programs depended upon serious civilian review. In addition, he brought in a number of skilled professionals who would provide direction for the Pentagon's administrative work during the years ahead.[16] Considering the budget limitations under which he operated, Forrestal's performance was praiseworthy.

Louis Johnson, Forrestal's successor, also came to the Defense Department with some previous experience in military affairs. One of the founders of the American Legion during the 1930s and also an assistant secretary of war between 1937 and 1940, Johnson was a practicing attorney who had long been involved in Democratic politics. His appointment as secretary of defense appeared to some observers as Truman's way of rewarding him for his fund-raising work during the 1948 campaign. They were not entirely wrong, although Johnson did possess a measure of civilian experience in military administration.

Johnson knew that Forrestal had lost Truman's support and that his own success in office depended on his ability to hold the confidence of the man in the White House. Truman clearly wanted greater economy at the Pentagon, the elimination of interservice feuding, and greater civilian coordination of the department's activities. Not a reluctant or timid man, Johnson aggressively set out to tame the Pentagon. Unlike Forrestal, however, Johnson had not been active in the government during World War II and did not witness the enormous changes which occurred in the defense establishment during that period. He had resigned as assistant secretary of war in 1940, when Roosevelt chose Henry Stimson to replace Harry Woodring as the secretary of war. His lack of experience and knowledge of the Pentagon's new personalities and policies placed him at a distinct disadvantage. Johnson's liabilities as secretary of defense became evident soon after he took office and created another problem for Truman.

Johnson began his tenure at the Defense Department inauspiciously. Failing to digest adequately Forrestal's final written briefing memorandum, he appeared uninformed and ill-prepared at his first news conference. To show the military "who was boss," he ordered the Army staff out of their space in Room 3E880 at the Pentagon, the office area reserved for the defense secretary.[17] (Forrestal had simply moved into a vacant office when he became defense secretary, leaving the Army staff where they were.) He regularly chastised military staff officers for what he believed were inadequate briefing presentations, an action which did much to lose him the respect and confidence of the military. He also slashed away at the internal departmental committee structure established by Forrestal and placed some of his former American Legion friends on his staff. Such cronyism angered the many disciples of Forrestal still at work in the department and provoked unflattering comparisons between Johnson and his predecessor.

Although Johnson certainly had his difficulties in the relatively routine matter of working with the Pentagon staff personnel, his major problems came when his policies brought about a revolt against his leadership by the military. Johnson's policy differences with the military began in April 1949, when he ordered a stop to naval construction. His action meant a halt to work on the Navy's flush-deck aircraft carrier, the *United States.* Just the previous week, the Navy had completed keel-laying ceremonies for the ship, and John L. Sullivan, the Navy secretary, appealed to Truman to countermand Johnson's order. Truman upheld Johnson's decision, however, and Sullivan angrily resigned with a public blast at the secretary of defense.[18]

The Navy's response to Johnson's decision soon developed into what observers referred to as the "Revolt of the Admirals," a year-long interservice feud between the Navy and Air Force that seriously weakened Johnson's credibility in Congress and the administration. Taken in retaliation for what some observers believed was Johnson's cutback in naval construction and his alleged partiality to Air Force views in strategic policy matters, the revolt was the Navy's method of dealing with a defense secretary who was unable to support its military objectives. The Navy conducted a public relations campaign throughout 1949 against the B-36, a long-range bomber developed (with a history of bad management) by the Air Force, maintaining that its own P2V aircraft performed better. It set about to prove its claim by staging test flights and submitting articles critical of Air Force aviation to popular magazines such as the *Reader's Digest* and the *Saturday Evening Post.* The Air Force responded with a public relations display of its own. When the Navy circulated an "Anonymous Document" accusing Johnson and Air Force Secretary Stuart Symington of malfeasance in office, Carl Vinson, the chairman of the House Armed Services Committee, called for an investigation of the nation's military program. Vinson's hearings lasted throughout the summer of 1949, and no evidence of wrongdoing by Johnson came out in the testimony. Nevertheless, the nation witnessed the sorry spectacle of a military establishment divided against itself and its civilian leadership.[19]

Johnson's standing continued to fall even after his vote of confidence (of sorts) from Carl Vinson. Truman continued to press for economy, and Johnson responded by closing several military installations and reducing payrolls. At the same time, however, the administration was conducting a review of its overall strategic policy. Truman had placed Secretary of State Dean Acheson in charge, and it was widely expected that Acheson's recommendations would determine the future direction of national security policy. The eventual product of his work was NSC-68, the planning document which called for a buildup of American military strength and a dramatic increase in military expenditures. Johnson learned of Acheson's plans in March 1950, and immediately objected to them. Fearful that NSC-68's security requirements would damage his economy drive at the Pentagon and harm his standing with the president, Johnson indicated his displeasure to Acheson. Truman, however, supported Acheson's work and left Johnson with only a feud between himself and the secretary of state.[20] As events soon proved, Johnson could ill afford such a bureaucratic dispute.

With the outbreak of the Korean hostilities in June 1950 and the early retreats by American forces in Korea, Truman's political critics blamed Johnson for the nation's supposed lack of preparedness. As the fighting grew more intense during the summer, Johnson began to differ with Acheson over the conduct of the war and their split widened. At the root of their dispute, logically enough, was General Douglas MacArthur. In August, MacArthur visited Formosa and held a series of conferences with Generalissimo Chiang Kai-shek. In clear violation of the administration's policy, MacArthur seemed to be moving toward an involvement of Chiang and his troops in the Korean War.

On 25 August, MacArthur sent a message to the annual convention of the Veterans of Foreign Wars in which he analyzed the importance of Formosa to the American military position in the Far East and implied that his critics in the administration were appeasing the enemy. At a meeting attended by Johnson and Acheson, Truman immediately demanded that Johnson order MacArthur to retract the statement. The secretary of defense, however, temporized and failed to follow the president's instructions. Shortly after leaving the meeting, Johnson telephoned Acheson to suggest that they weaken Truman's statement to suggest that MacArthur's message was simply "one man's opinion and not the official policy of the United States government."[21] Acheson wanted no part of Johnson's suggestion, feeling that Truman had made clear what he expected of the secretary of defense.

Truman realized by September 1950 that Johnson's position in the cabinet was untenable. Unable to work with Acheson, Johnson became involved in a partisan intrigue with Robert Taft, the Republican leader in the Senate, for the secretary of state's dismissal. Earlier policy differences with Acheson over the direction of the defense program and the development of the hydrogen bomb grew into personal attacks by Johnson on the loyalty of State Department personnel. Acheson later recalled: "Johnson's behavior had passed from the peculiar to the impossible."[22] Later in the month, Truman called Johnson to the White House and requested his resignation. It was a step Truman had to take; his own political advisers warned him that Johnson's continued presence would cost the party votes in November. In his resignation statement, a shocked Louis Johnson recommended that George Catlett Marshall be appointed as his successor.[23]

Marshall's appointment gave Truman and Acheson a sense of tremendous relief. Marshall's immense prestige and ability provided the office with a much-needed measure of respect. Both Marshall and his successor, Robert Lovett, faced responsibilities in the position that were different from those of their predecessors, however. The military requirements of the Korean War made Truman's earlier demands for economy in the defense budget somewhat irrelevant. The major priority for the Defense Department was the resolution of the Korean conflict, with secondary importance attached to the upgrading of the defense establishment for the arming of the nation's treaty allies in Europe. The Pentagon budget virtually tripled between 1950 and 1952 as the United States strained to meet its new military commitments.

Marshall's tenure as secretary of defense lasted only one year, but taking immediate command of mobilization, he brought administrative order to the war effort. Furthermore, Marshall's presence at the Pentagon helped to restore some discipline to the department's administrative work. Johnson's staff personnel were replaced by more experienced men. Unlike Johnson, Marshall never tongue-lashed ineffective subordinates, but found quieter ways (usually a transfer to another area of work) of dealing with individuals whose work failed to satisfy his expectations. Acheson especially found Marshall's return to the cabinet profitable. Interagency committees comprised of State Department, Defense Department, and executive branch personnel were established to coordinate national security policy. Marshall's testimony in Congress supporting increased forces in Europe helped to bring about a military commitment to the newly formed North Atlantic Treaty Organization.[24]

The war in Korea and the behavior of General MacArthur continued to plague both the Truman administration and Secretary Marshall throughout 1950 and 1951, however. MacArthur's successful offensive after the Inchon landing placed the United Nations' forces in a position to press the attack. When MacArthur invaded North Korea in October and moved farther up the peninsula, however, Communist Chinese forces intervened in great numbers, inflicting defeats upon the UN troops, who retreated to South Korea. Chagrined by these defeats, MacArthur wanted to strike directly at Chinese bases in Manchuria. Truman refused to permit such an expansion of the war, and the frustrated MacArthur flared into open insubordination during the winter of 1950 and the spring of 1951. In April, Truman made the highly controversial decision to replace MacArthur with General Matthew Ridgway. MacArthur's abrupt dismissal created a political uproar in the United States, and MacArthur later claimed that Marshall acquiesced in his firing because of a past personal jealousy. In the subsequent hearings in the Senate on MacArthur's dismissal, Marshall strengthened the administration's position with his presence and his testimony that the general had "grown far out of sympathy with the established policies of the government." But MacArthur's supporters in the military establishment began a gossipy smear campaign against the secretary of defense which continued until Marshall left office in September 1951.[25]

Robert Lovett was a defense secretary in the Forrestal-Marshall mold. Like Forrestal, he was an investment banker before entering government service during World War II. Later he had been Marshall's associate as undersecretary of state and deputy secretary of defense. Like both Forrestal and Marshall, he took a generalist view of the responsibilities of the secretary of defense and became involved in the total national security policy-making process. Lovett's relations with the other members of Truman's cabinet were positive, and he also worked well with Pentagon administrators. Following Marshall's lead, Lovett continued the policy coordination between the State and

Defense departments. He developed sound working relations with Acheson, and Pentagon staffers appreciated his reasonable approach to departmental work. His ability as a negotiator contrasted favorably with the autocratic style of Louis Johnson.[26]

Although he was largely occupied with the Korean War effort, Lovett detected some organizational problems in Pentagon administration during his tenure. His knowledge of federal budgeting processes was extensive, and he sought to redirect the Defense Department fiscal operations from an annual to a long-term approach. Like his predecessors, he believed that the defense secretary's authority to supervise the military needed strengthening. Mindful of the inefficiency of the Pentagon's procurement procedures, he recommended an administrative reorganization which would provide for an improved management structure.[27]

Lovett's service in the Truman administration was physically and mentally exhausting. Some time later, he would tell President-elect John F. Kennedy that the Defense Department was "an empire too great for any emperor." This "monstrosity," had brought him to the verge of collapse, and he was hospitalized after his term in office ended.[28] The problems of his office, as well as the reforms which he had recommended, were to become the property of his successor, Charles E. Wilson.

Unlike his predecessors, Wilson had no formal military career, and he had never held a defense-related position in government. As the president of General Motors Corporation between 1941 and 1953, however, he had supervised several billion dollars worth of military production for the government. During World War II, for instance, Wilson oversaw the production of over $10 billion in war material, and he regularly testified in Congress on the corporation's defense effort. At the time of his appointment as secretary of defense, Wilson was acknowledged to be one of the nation's outstanding production specialists. Furthermore, the fact that he had served as president of the nation's largest industrial enterprise for twelve years indicated that he could manage a large and complex organization. Although previous defense secretaries had spent a considerable portion of their time developing national security policy, many observers believed that the secretary should pay more attention to improving the administra-

Secretary-designate Wilson, President-elect Dwight D. Eisenhower, and military leaders in South Korea in December 1952. Left to right: General James A. Van Fleet; Major John Eisenhower; Wilson; General Omar Bradley; General Mark Clark; Eisenhower.

By permission of the Wilson Archives

tive proficiency of the department. Given those sentiments, Wilson was a logical choice for the post because of his managerial achievements.[29]

Wilson had shown an interest in the problems of the Defense Department as early as 1949 and he may have regarded his life's experiences as training for the role which Eisenhower had outlined for him in 1952.[30] Born in Minerva, Ohio, in 1890, Wilson spent his boyhood and school years in Pittsburgh. Always interested in things mechanical, Wilson struck up a boyhood friendship with the Diebolt brothers, two engineers on the local railroad, who showed him how the new Westinghouse air-braking system operated. His curiosity and intelligence combined to make him an outstanding student. He graduated from high school at the age of sixteen, having passed over two grades, and enrolled in the Carnegie Institute of Technology in 1906, finishing the normal four-year course in three years. Graduating in 1909 among the top five scholars in his class, he was nicknamed "Wizard" by his classmates because he could solve integral calculus problems without committing the equations to paper.[31]

After graduation, Wilson took his first position in private industry as an engineering apprentice at the Westinghouse Company. At Westinghouse, he worked for over two years under B. J. Lamme, known throughout the industry as one of the finest electrical engineers in the world. The young Wilson's work at Westinghouse proved outstanding; he designed the company's first electrical ignition for automobiles and, during World War I, turned down a captain's commission in the Army in order to work on dynamotor devices for aircraft. When Wilson left Westinghouse in 1919, he discovered that Lamme had kept evaluations of the forty-eight apprentices who had worked under him. They received marks in six different areas: analytical ability, initiative, originality and resourcefulness, executive ability, accuracy and reliability, and personality. Lamme's overall evaluation of Wilson placed him at the head of the list.[32]

After the war, Wilson contacted Alfred P. Sloan, one of the major executive officers at General Motors, about a job with this emerging automobile business. Impressed by Wilson, Sloan found the young engineer a temporary position in Detroit in 1919. Wilson took a transfer later that year to Anderson, Indiana, where he became the chief engineer and sales manager of Remy Electric Company, a subsidiary of General Motors. During the 1920s, Wilson helped increase the company's profits and also assisted in the acquisition of several smaller concerns for the parent corporation. In 1929, Wilson became a vice-president at General Motors and succeeded William Knudsen as president in 1941.

Two facets of Wilson's career at General Motors were especially significant: his production and planning ability and his contribution to the development of a labor relations policy. Wilson's production abilities became especially evident during World War II, when he directed an effort which turned out over $10 million worth of military equipment every day. Furthermore, his career had reached the point where he was satisfying a longstanding interest in the management of large organizations.[33] He made his mark in the labor relations area by becoming the first automobile executive to establish a true modus vivendi with Walter Reuther, the president of the United Auto Workers (UAW). Beset by labor difficulties both before and after World War II, General Motors needed a consistent policy. Wilson's response was twofold. First, he proposed the principle of the "escalator" clause and the annual improvement (or productivity) factor during the 1948 labor negotiations. The escalator clause tied wages to increases or declines in the cost of living and was the corporation's method of protecting workers from the postwar inflation. Second, Wilson proposed, in April 1950, the creation of a companywide pension plan for General Motors workers, the first major retirement offer in the history of the auto industry. The UAW agreed to Wilson's proposal in October 1950.[34] Thanks to these bargaining successes, Wilson and the UAW negotiated long-term contracts that kept the corporation free of major labor trouble until the mid-1950s. Wilson appears to have been an unusually competent negotiator, although he had critics both on the labor side and within the management of General Motors. One executive, who felt that Wilson's offers to the UAW were too generous, declared that "C.E.," the initials by which Wilson was known within the corporation, stood for "Compromise Everything" Wilson.[35]

Because Wilson was an individual with rather simple tastes and a pungent sense of humor, his serious contributions to the development of the automobile industry were sometimes overlooked. These circumstances repeated themselves during his tenure at the Pentagon, when his candor and humor made him appear somewhat misplaced among Washington's gray-flannel figures. Nevertheless, he did enjoy a highly successful career in an industry which stressed technological knowledge and managerial competence. These attributes were also necessary for anyone who expected to serve as the secretary of defense.

Wilson assumed responsibilities as Eisenhower's secretary of defense which were sharply different from those Truman had outlined for Forrestal, Johnson, Marshall, and Lovett. Eisenhower expected Wilson to bring administrative order to the Pentagon; Eisenhower and other administration officials of his choosing would develop broad strategy outlines while leaving Wilson with the serious responsibility of Pentagon management. This apparent divorce of strategic responsibility from managerial responsibility made Wilson's administrative tasks even more important. He chose to merge his corporate managerial training with the "practical wisdom" accumulated by his predecessors in an attempt to make the Pentagon better serve the defense needs of the country.[36]

One significant point should be stressed, however. Even though

Wilson adapted a business management technique to the resolution of defense problems, he never intended to run the Pentagon as he did General Motors, through a profit-loss, balance-sheet approach. Instead, his purpose involved what Peter F. Drucker has described as the difference between "effectiveness" and "efficiency."[37] Government departments are not businesses and cannot be expected to operate along the lines of "business efficiency," showing a profit at year's end. Government agencies, however, were often ineffective because they lacked the ability to clarify authority, define responsibility, set objectives, and evaluate performance. Wilson encountered a Pentagon bureaucracy in 1952 with authority split within the civilian and military leadership and responsibility unclear at many levels. To become effective (especially in peacetime), the Defense Department's organizational procedures needed redirection.

Wilson's major task became the management of that redirection process. Like other General Motors executives of his generation, Wilson learned his management lessons from Alfred P. Sloan, the longtime chairman. The pioneer of an organizational philosophy of centralized policy and decentralized administration, Sloan took General Motors to the leadership of the automotive industry through the use of administrative procedures whereby corporate officials made policy decisions and the various division heads exercised autonomy in the management of operations. Sloan's method became a model for other administrative structures because it invested control in the executive officers and provided freedom for the management. Wilson proposed to use this decentralized administrative approach in his efforts to increase the effectiveness of the Pentagon.

Wilson's managerial objectives played a central role in his importance to the administration. Wilson was not a "functionalist" defense secretary, however, at least in the sense that he merely carried out policy determined by Eisenhower and other administrators. To be sure, Eisenhower's views prevailed in the formulation of national defense policy. The president's thinking, however, often conflicted with that of the military and his political opposition in Congress. When such conflicts became a matter of public record, Wilson emerged as the administration's spokesman and responsible official on national defense policy. In such a capacity, he often became a man of controversy, a situation unusual for an official with mere functional responsibilities. He might more accurately be described as the executive in the Pentagon charged with the explanation, implementation, and public defense of the administration's national security policy. Although he had been interested in the management of large organizations since his college days, Wilson's greatest challenge lay ahead, with the inauguration of President Eisenhower.

3

The Furor over Confirmation

C HARLES E. Wilson expected his nomination as secretary of defense to encounter little opposition in the Senate. Even before undergoing confirmation hearings in January 1953, Wilson casually remarked, "I've got a feeling that I'm going to be pretty pleased and surprised at how easily those boys can be handled."[1] But the members of the Senate Armed Services Committee, the "boys" to whom Wilson referred, apparently had other ideas once they began to examine his candidacy. Unlike the other members of Eisenhower's first cabinet, Wilson found that his confirmation was postponed until he made certain adjustments in his personal finances. His confirmation proved difficult and was the first political test for the incoming administration.

Wilson's confirmation or rejection as secretary of defense depended on his willingness to part with his vast private holdings in General Motors. At the time of his confirmation hearings on 15, 16, and 23 January 1953, Wilson owned 39,470 shares of stock in the corporation. His wife, Jessie, also held a substantial interest in General Motors, and the Wilsons' combined holdings totaled almost 50,000 shares. Furthermore, Wilson belonged to a corporate bonus and salary plan which entitled him to cash and stock awards over the next four years.[2] Such vast holdings raised concern over a possible conflict of interest between Wilson's public position as defense secretary and his private financial interests in General Motors. The nation's largest automaker was also one of the Pentagon's major contractors. As secretary of defense, Wilson might have to decide on contractual awards involving public expenditures which could have a significant effect on his private fortune.

The dilemma over Wilson's nomination and his stock holdings was complex even before partisan politics intruded to complicate it further. At issue were not only Wilson's substantial wealth but also the qualifications of businessmen for public service and the integrity of the Senate's responsibility to advise and consent on presidential nominees. One may view Wilson's confirmation difficulties as important only to the events of January 1953. Later events seemed to prove, however, that this problem represented the first test of strength between the Eisenhower administration and its congressional opposition.

Wilson was not the only member of the first Eisenhower cabinet whose background was in the business world. Indeed, eight of the nine men nominated had previously held executive positions in large business concerns or had been connected to big business through corporate law practices. For example, Eisenhower chose George M. Humphrey, formerly chairman of M. A. Hanna and Company, as secretary of the treasury, and John Foster Dulles and Herbert Brownell, corporate lawyers from New York, as secretary of state and attorney general respectively. The corporate flavor of the Eisenhower cabinet was so pronounced that TRB acidly commented in the *New Republic* that "eight millionaires and a plumber" would be determining national policy for the next four years.[3]

On the surface, these nominations appeared to be Eisenhower's way of rewarding the business community for its support during the 1952 campaign. Furthermore, it was known that Eisenhower admired successful businessmen and agreed with their generally conservative belief in the free enterprise system. More than political rewards were involved in Wilson's nomination as secretary of defense, however. Eisenhower wanted a skilled industrial manager who could efficiently administer the burgeoning Pentagon operation and make it conform to his administration's overall economic objectives. Wilson's past experience at General Motors made him a prime candidate to assume this role. In fact, Eisenhower and Wilson had known each other for several years and even corresponded between 1947 and 1952.[4] Wilson was much in demand as a public lecturer and regularly sent

Eisenhower copies of his prepared remarks on national defense, economic policy, and labor-management relations. Eisenhower's previous military experience caused him to believe that the Defense Department needed a change in administrative direction or else its insatiable desire for the public dollar could bring the nation to the verge of bankruptcy. After Lucius Clay, the president-elect's chief cabinet recruiter, concurred with Eisenhower's assessment of Wilson's managerial abilities, it was apparent that Wilson would be nominated. Eisenhower later gave his reasons for the appointment in *Mandate for Change*: "[Mr. Wilson] had a reputation as one of the ablest of our executives in big corporations. I sought an experienced man of this kind because of the huge procurement, storage, transportation, distribution, and other logistical functions of the Defense Department."[5]

By stressing Wilson's managerial and administrative expertise, Eisenhower revealed that strategic policy matters would be primarily handled by other members of the administration. His emphasis on the secretary of defense's role as supervisor and administrator was an abrupt departure from Truman's preference for involving the secretary in political, military, foreign policy, and strategic matters. Wilson's predecessors, especially Forrestal, Marshall, and Lovett, had all been actively involved in strategic planning. Even so, Wilson's nomination met with almost unanimous approval when it was announced on 20 November 1952. The *Christian Science Monitor* agreed with Eisenhower's belief that the Defense Department needed "business efficiency," and the *Washington Post* labeled Wilson "a wise choice."[6]

The Senate Armed Services Committee began to examine Wilson's nomination in mid-January 1953, and it soon became evident that the senators had differences of opinion, as to how Wilson should resolve his potential conflict of interest problem and also as to the wisdom of Eisenhower's reliance on the business community for cabinet positions. Republicans privately joined Democrats in expressing concern about the big-business nature of the prospective administration. Robert Taft, the Senate's most influential Republican, was especially critical of Eisenhower's choices. "The way things have come out," he grumped, "it looks to me as if the government cars hereafter will be Chevrolets."[7]

"It's Not Customary, Mr. Wilson"

From *Herblock's Here and Now* (Simon & Schuster, 1955)

One Way to Help Balance the Budget

By permission of *The Washington Star*

When Wilson appeared before the Armed Services Committee on 15 January 1953, he discovered that his session with this group of senators was not going to be as simple as he had originally believed. At issue was the manner in which he intended to comply with Section 434, Title 18 (1863) of the United States Code, prohibiting a "government official directly or indirectly involved in the pecuniary profits of a corporation" from transacting "business with it as an agent of the government." That regulation, at the time nearly ninety years old, seemed to demand that Wilson part with his stock. Yet many individuals with substantial investments had previously entered government service (especially during wartime) and retained their private holdings. Normal procedure in such instances required that an individual announce his resignation from his corporation and stipulate that a noninterested third party would handle any business between his former company and the federal authority. Wilson almost certainly recalled the case of William T. Knudsen, his predecessor as the president of General Motors, who resigned from the corporation to supervise the nation's pre-World War II conversion and mobilization tasks.[8]

There were two recent instances, however, where key Defense Department personnel had divested themselves of their private interests before entering government service. Stuart Symington, secretary of the air force under President Truman and in 1953 a senator from Missouri, had paid a $67,000 capital gains tax in the divestiture of his stock in 1947 when he assumed his position at the Pentagon. Louis Johnson had also sold his shares in Convair aircraft before being confirmed as the second secretary of defense in 1949.[9] Wilson's fate depended upon whether the Senate Armed Services Committee interpreted the language of the code strictly.

In examining Wilson, the senators focused on two matters. First, was there any likelihood that Wilson could use his public position as secretary of defense to increase his personal wealth by awarding immense defense contracts to General Motors? Second, how effective a public official could Wilson become when he had spent his entire adult career in the private sector? The Pentagon was not a profit-making organization; could Wilson adapt his thinking to the requirements of a public policy position? Wilson attempted to assure the committee that he would not be involved in any conflict of interest by announcing his resignation from General Motors and explaining that other Pentagon officials would handle contractual negotiations involving the corporation and the Defense Department. He did not, however, intend to sell his stock in General Motors because he would then be liable for a sizable capital gains tax.

Republican members of the Armed Services Committee were inclined to support Wilson's solution of the problem. The leading Republicans on the committee, Chairman Leverett Saltonstall (Mass.)

and Styles Bridges (N.H.), accepted the resignation plus disqualification procedure outlined by the candidate. Saltonstall, one of Eisenhower's major supporters in the Senate, wanted this issue settled in committee in order to avoid any embarrassment for the president-elect.[10] Democrats on the Armed Services Committee, however, were not inclined to be as generous with Wilson as their Republican counterparts. When Lyndon Johnson, Stuart Symington, and Richard Russell began their questioning, the hearings livened considerably. Senator Johnson was the first to be "bothered" by Wilson's private holdings and suggested that the nominee divest himself of his securities in order to avoid public apprehension. Wilson informed Johnson that the capital gains tax involved in such a transaction "was too great, and I do not know why you should ask me to do it."[11] Symington's questioning followed the same path as Johnson's.

The probing of his personal finances disturbed Wilson, and he soon realized that the hearings were going poorly. When Senator Robert Hendrickson (R.-N.J.) offered him the time to clarify his testimony, Wilson jumped at the opportunity. Matters quickly grew worse, however, after the two men participated in the following exchange:

Hendrickson: If a situation did arise where you had to make a decision that was extremely adverse to the interest of your own stock and General Motors. . . . in the interest of the United States government, could you make that decision?

Wilson: Yes, sir, I could. I cannot conceive of one because for years I thought that what was good for our country was good for General Motors and vice versa. The difference does not exist. Our company is too big. It goes with the welfare of the nation. Our contribution to the nation is quite considerable.[12]

With that statement, Wilson turned the hearings into a Washington conversation piece. Although the statement has been quoted in different ways, a reading of the transcript shows that he did not say, "What's good for General Motors is good for the country." Indeed, he stated that "what was good for our country was good for General Motors"; and by "vice versa," he implied that what was bad for the country was also bad for General Motors.[13]

Considering that misleading and sometimes contradictory versions of Wilson's testimony reached the press, the public received a distorted interpretation of his remarks. Wilson, however, apparently saw no reason why his statement should create any controversy. During World War II, Wilson supervised defense production for General Motors and occasionally testified before Congress on the corporation's wartime performance as well as about its plans for the postwar period. On 24 May 1943, he told the Colmer Committee, the congressional group studying postwar economic planning, that General Motors was not placing its interests ahead of the nation as a whole.

We think this in General Motors: that our business is so tied up with the lives of the people, so important to their doing things in the American way, and having the standard of living that we have established in this country, that we cannot conceive how our company can be prosperous when the country isn't prosperous. So we say what is good for our country is good for General Motors. I think we get along pretty well with that point of view. I happen to think General Motors is one of the great democratic institutions in America. The principles on which we operate are consistent with our country's principles. Sometimes people do not understand us.[14]

Later in 1943, Wilson appeared before the Senate Committee to Investigate the National Defense Program, popularly known after its chairman, Senator Harry S. Truman of Missouri. Asked by Senator James Mead (D.-N.Y.) if the postwar plans of General Motors took into account the economic well-being of the United States, Wilson replied:

Well, we have a very simple point of view in General Motors. We think that what is good for the country is good for us. We don't have any separate kind of position. We think we are so big, the products we make are so vitally associated with the welfare of the citizens, that we say that what's good for the country we go along with, and that is good for us.

In testimony before other congressional committees, Wilson again had compared the national welfare to that of General Motors, always placing country ahead of corporation. No senator or congressman found fault with his comparison; Senator Mead even endorsed Wilson's comments.[15] Under those circumstances, Wilson felt no reluctance in 1953 in making a similar statement.

The hearings on Wilson's nomination were conducted in executive session. When reporters began to assemble the isolated bits and pieces of testimony provided by those who were present, they discovered that Wilson's statement was a political bombshell. News of Wilson's linkage of General Motors with the national welfare produced an immediate controversy. The *Washington Evening Star,* usually sympathetic to Republicans, caustically remarked: "It was a mistake to name Charles E. Wilson to head the Department of Defense. Even if he gave up his financial connections, he could scarcely quit thinking as his fellow industrialists think." Amused by Wilson's predicament, the traditionally Democratic *New York Post* rumored that Eisenhower intended to withdraw the nomination and replace Wilson with Lucius Clay.[16] With the nominee unconfirmed, Saltonstall adjourned the hearings on 16 January, wishing to spare Eisenhower any future embarrassment. Before the president-elect had spent one day in office, this unusual controversy over a cabinet nominee already threatened the credibility of the first Republican administration since the Great Depression.

For several days, Wilson pondered his fate and tried to determine why his nomination was in jeopardy. He had clearly failed to impress the committee with his political views or his method of avoiding a conflict of interest. Some senators were also irritated by Wilson's blunt yet loquacious style of testimony. Especially irksome was his habit of referring to the senators as "you men," a colloquialism Wilson also used in addressing corporate colleagues, labor leaders, reporters, and even his church's men's association.[17] This rhetorical habit, long a Wilson trademark, impressed some senators as the candidate's way of lecturing them. For his part, Wilson probably saw no problem with this manner of speaking, and he certainly meant no disrespect to the committee. He had, in fact, used the phrase thirteen separate times when testifying before the Colmer and Truman committees in 1943.

Wilson's difficulties caused the Republican leadership serious concern. Eisenhower, Saltonstall, and several of the president-elect's aides began to urge the candidate to sell his stock. The Republican congressional leadership, including Senator Taft, understood that no changes could be enacted in the conflict of interest statute while Wilson was under consideration, and there seemed little likelihood that Wilson would be permitted to enter the administration with his portfolio intact. Unwilling to withdraw the nomination and thereby lose some necessary political momentum, Eisenhower bluntly informed Wilson on the night of the inauguration that he would have to sell his stock if he expected to serve as secretary of defense.[18] Wilson wanted to sleep on his decision and scheduled a conference with the president at the White House for the following afternoon.

On the morning after the inauguration, Saltonstall called on Wilson at his hotel and requested him to follow Eisenhower's advice. Wilson refused, however, and instead informed the senator of his displeasure with the course of the hearings. Angry at what he considered the excessive probing of his finances and intentions, Wilson told Saltonstall that he had always acted responsibly in his previous dealings with the government. He declined to sell his stock simply because of pressure from the Democrats. Saltonstall unhappily concluded his visit and prepared for future problems with the committee. However, Saltonstall's disappointment was short-lived. On the afternoon of 21 January, Wilson informed the president that he intended to sell his stock. The divestiture would include his present holdings in General Motors as well as the money due him from his unearned and undelivered bonus. According to the terms of his agreement with the corporation, Wilson could make no change in the terms of his bonus until the stipulated cash and stock benefits became his possession. Saltonstall received preliminary notice of Wilson's decision before James Hagerty, Eisenhower's press secretary, made the formal announcement on 22 January. The hearings on Wilson's nomination resumed on 23 January.[19]

Wilson opened the second stage of the hearings with a statement explaining the procedure which he intended to follow in selling the stock.

> In order to achieve this objective [confirmation], I have decided after carefully considering the matter, to dispose of all the General Motors stocks which I now own and any which I am entitled in the future.
>
> If . . . I must deal with any matter of business which I may feel might be the subject of misunderstanding on account of my previous relationship with General Motors Corporation, I have been assured of discussing the matter personally with the President.

After some further questioning, Wilson revealed that his sale of stock would take approximately thirty days. He gave a commitment to finish the sale by 1 April.[20]

But the simple sale of the stock failed to satisfy certain committee Democrats, who wondered how Wilson proposed to handle his unearned and undelivered bonus. At this point, the hearings took another dramatic turn, and the secretary-designate found himself on the defensive once again.

Wilson's bonus had been of only minor importance until the second stage of the hearings. The candidate was entitled to a bonus award, consisting of cash and stock, for his past service with General Motors. It would be paid in installments from 1953 to 1957; only if he performed "contrary to the interests of General Motors" would those benefits be denied.[21] Two parts of the bonus plan concerned the Democratic membership of the Armed Services Committee. First, what was the exact meaning of the phrase, "contrary to the interests of General Motors?" Wilson explained that if he worked for one of the competitors of General Motors, such as the Ford Motor Company or the Chrysler Corporation, he could lose his bonus. The plan was meant to prevent capable executives from auctioning off their services to the highest bidder in the industry. Participation in a lucrative bonus arrangement with his corporation provided an executive with an incentive to remain with his employer. Some senators implied that the phrase might be construed to mean that Wilson, as secretary of defense, might lose his benefits if he awarded an expensive contract to one of General Motors' rivals. Wilson argued that the language of his agreement with the corporation precluded such an interpretation. Unconvinced, Senators Johnson and Russell inquired whether it might be more appropriate for Wilson to sell the stock portion of the award before becoming secretary of defense. Wilson repeated his earlier claim that no amount of the bonus could be transferred until it became his own property.

With the hearings deadlocked once again, Senator Harry F. Byrd (D.-Va.) came to Wilson's assistance. An Eisenhower supporter, Byrd had previously alerted the president to the problems which Wilson's finances presented to the committee. Byrd asked the candidate to repeat his intentions regarding the settlement of the bonus award.

Byrd: Will you permit [me] just to clear one thing very definitely? As soon as you receive this stock, Mr. Wilson, as part of your bonus, you will sell it immediately?

Wilson: I will sell it immediately.

Byrd: I just want to make one thing clear for the record that he can't sell the stock until he receives it, but as soon as he does, he will sell it.[22]

The Wilson-Byrd understanding failed to satisfy Richard Russell, however. The ranking Democrat on the Armed Services Committee, Russell argued that Wilson's decisions as secretary of defense could conceivably raise the value of General Motors securities. Claiming that the potential for future abuses existed, Russell demanded that Wilson pledge to sell the stock portion of his bonus prior to becoming secretary of defense. Again citing the legal impossibility of Russell's proposal, Wilson stated that the law forbade him to change any terms of his agreement with General Motors without the consent of the corporation's stockholders. To allay Russell's suspicions, Wilson offered to give any part of the stock portion of the bonus which increased its market value to charity. Russell persisted in his questioning, however, and Wilson took offense at the senator's implication that he might act dishonestly. The atmosphere in the conference room grew especially tense when Wilson and Russell exchanged the following remarks:

Russell: Have you exhausted every effort to see whether you can dispose of it?

Wilson: I know what you are talking about, but I really feel that you are giving me quite a pushing around. If I had come here to cheat, I wouldn't be here.

Russell: I'm sorry you feel that way, Mr. Wilson. I am not trying to push you around, but I have my responsibilities, too.

Wilson: I understand that. But I am just human and I am making a great sacrifice to come down here.

Decidedly provoked, Wilson probably cared little about his nomination after his confrontation with Russell. In his opinion, the senators were asking hypothetical questions which hardly related to his qualifications for the position. When Senator John Sherman Cooper (R.-Ky.) began his questioning, Wilson icily told him, "I am beginning to think that you would be doing me a great favor if you do not" approve the nomination.[23]

With another roadblock in the path of Wilson's confirmation, long-suffering Leverett Saltonstall urged a temporary adjournment of the morning's proceedings. During the recess, Wilson conferred with the legal counsel of the General Motors Bonus and Salary Committee. Agreeing that his situation presented an extraordinary circumstance, the counsel recommended that the stock portion of Wilson's bonus be converted into cash at the current market value. Wilson presented the counsel's opinion to the Armed Services Committee when it resumed its deliberations. Satisfied that he had finally met its requirements, the committee unanimously recommended his candidacy.[24]

Wilson's nomination encountered modest opposition when it reached the floor of the Senate. Wayne Morse, the very independent Republican from Oregon, led the anti-Wilson group, which also included Democrats Paul Douglas, Herbert Lehman, Olin Johnston, Harley Kilgore, Matthew Neely, and Willis Smith. Morse referred to Wilson as "a man lacking the nth degree of ethical standards."[25] Few other senators seemed to share his sentiments, however, as Wilson was confirmed by a margin of 77-6. He had passed his first major ordeal with the Senate.

Wilson's confirmation did not end the administration's difficulties with the Armed Services Committee, however. The secretary's civilian appointees still required Senate approval, and their status was also questionable. All of Wilson's nominees for armed service secretaries—Robert Stevens, Robert Anderson, and Harold Talbott—held sizable private investments. Stevens, who was to head the Army, was formerly president of J. P. Stevens, the major textile manufacturer. Anderson, chosen as secretary of the navy, was a prominent Texas attorney with interests in the securities, agriculture, and energy fields. Talbott, associated with Dayton-Wright Aircraft, was Wilson's choice as secretary of the air force. Wilson also brought Roger Kyes, a vice-president at General Motors, with him to Washington as the deputy secretary of defense. Each of Wilson's lieutenants faced rigorous questioning from the committee regarding the disposition of their personal finances. Anderson encountered the least difficulty, while Stevens, Kyes, and Talbott found "rough sledding" in their hearings. Eventually Wilson's advisers followed his example and sold their private holdings. The secretary of defense intended to prevent any recurrence of this difficult episode; his first official act was to bar any Pentagon official from negotiating with a firm in which he had previously held an interest.[26]

New Top Man On The Pentagon Totem Pole

By permission of *The Washington Star*

Wilson's problems with the Armed Services Committee require an analysis which extends beyond mere description of the political controversy caused by the hearings. Contemporary newspaper accounts split pretty much along party lines, with the pro-Republican publications praising the secretary and the pro-Democratic ones criticizing the administration.[27] The historian, however, has to ask how a relatively routine confirmation hearing developed into a full-blown political confrontation between the administration and its emerging congressional opposition. Was Wilson treated differently by members of the Armed Services Committee from Eisenhower's other business-oriented nominees when they underwent confirmation hearings before their respective committees? In short, was Wilson singled out for political attack?

The transcript of the hearings demonstrates that both Wilson and his critics on the committee contributed to an embarrassing situation. Wilson failed to prepare himself adequately for his appearance, and although a change in his personal style and manner may not have been necessary, he could have helped his candidacy by a stricter observance of Senate customs and procedures. His periodic displays of impatience with the senators' questioning also damaged his relations with the committee. Yet it is important to remember that Wilson followed the committee's expressed wishes through the sale of his stock. Admittedly, Wilson agreed reluctantly to the divestiture and tended to view it as an example of partisanship rather than as the serious conflict of interest issue maintained by some senators.[28] For its part, the committee's Democratic membership persistently opposed Wilson's nomination even after he declared his full intention to follow the law. Johnson and Russell pressed Wilson to sell the stock portion of his bonus before he owned it, implying (at least in Wilson's mind) that he might act dishonestly in the meantime. Wilson's previous record in cooperating with the federal government was impeccable; he was understandably angered when the senators refused to trust his judgment on this complex issue.

Eisenhower and Wilson seemed to believe that the secretary of defense had been a target for political attack during his confirmation hearings.[29] Indeed, except for Wilson, the president's business-oriented nominees had no difficulty gaining Senate approval. George M. Humphrey, for example, nominated by Eisenhower to head the Treasury Department, was a wealthy businessman-industrialist who, like Wilson, held sizable private investments. Eisenhower's preference for delegating authority to cabinet members ensured that Humphrey would become an exceptionally influential member of the administration. After a short time, Humphrey emerged as Eisenhower's primary economic spokesman as well as an individual who influenced policy on taxation, federal spending levels, foreign trade, budgetary allocations, and other issues. In a real sense, Humphrey's economic decisions affected the profits of companies in which he held investments.

Humphrey testified on his nomination before the Senate Finance

Wilson at his swearing-in as secretary of defense on 28 January 1953. Left to right: Wilson; President Dwight D. Eisenhower; Frank C. Anderson, administrative officer at the White House.

By permission of the Wilson Archives

Committee on 19 January 1953. In his opening statement, he explained his previous employment as the chairman of the M. A. Hanna Company, a major industrial operation located in Ohio. The company was active in coal, iron ore, and steel production, with additional interests in shipbuilding and transportation. Humphrey realized that a possible conflict of interest might exist between his public duties as treasury secretary and his private holdings in M. A. Hanna, yet he still intended to retain his stock while serving in the Eisenhower administration. He outlined the procedure by which he hoped to avoid any conflict of interest by informing the committee:

I am advised by counsel that there is no legal reason why I should not continue to hold the securities I now own.

I shall, of course, advise my immediate assistants [at the Treasury Department] to see to it that I have no participation in the decision of any case or transaction involving any of the companies in which, through stock ownership, I am directly or indirectly interested.

I think that sets forth my position as briefly and as pointedly as I am able to do it.

My understanding is that there is a legal ruling that the ownership of stock in a corporation is not directly or indirectly engaging in business.[30]

Like Wilson, Humphrey intended to disqualify himself on matters where his public responsibilities and private investments may have conflicted. Like Wilson, Humphrey faced some issues concerning which conflicts might have developed. Prior to being nominated for the treasury post, Humphrey represented the M. A. Hanna Company before Congress to urge American participation in the construction of the Saint Lawrence Seaway. Although he had supported the construction of the seaway, Humphrey nevertheless persuaded the Finance Committee that he could retain his stock and still deal objectively with the seaway issue as a member of the administration. Members of the committee did request Humphrey to clarify his views on the matter. Committee Chairman Eugene Millikin (R.-Colo.) asked the candidate specifically if he intended to use his influence to encourage legislation for the Saint Lawrence Seaway. Humphrey responded:

Well, Senator, I think I can answer the whole thing in one word, and I think it just stands to reason. If I were trying to advance the interests of any of these companies, I don't believe I would be here at all and I don't believe anybody would think I would be here at all.

It is perfectly obvious, if I were trying to advance my own interests or the interests of the companies as against anyone else, I would stay with them.

I am here for just one purpose and that is to try to do a job for our country.[31]

The matter of Humphrey's private holdings worried the Finance Committee, but the senators still approved his nomination after the one-day session. Humphrey seemed little concerned about the likelihood of any conflict of interest. When Senator Robert Kerr (D.-Okla.) warned him of the discretionary problems presented by his investments, Humphrey dismissed that concern by stating, "You [can] get yourself into a position where if you do not be practical. . . . you cannot have a Secretary of the Treasury unless he is a man who has nothing."[32]

On close inspection, the confirmation cases of Wilson and Humphrey look remarkably similar. Both men were prominent industrialists who wanted to retain their private investments while serving in the Eisenhower administration. Based on their understanding of federal law, both intended to refer any matter which might involve a conflict of interest to subordinates for final decisions. Both entered government service for the expressed purpose of "doing a job for the country"; if they wished to increase their personal fortunes, they would have remained at their positions in industry. As each man's testimony bore out, they felt that their reputations attested to their integrity. They therefore regarded senatorial concern over possible future indiscretions as excessive, impractical, and unfair.

There was, of course, one significant difference between the candidacies of the two men. While the Finance Committee approved Humphrey in virtually pro forma fashion, the Armed Services Committee extended hearings on Wilson's nomination for over a week before granting approval. Senator Harry Byrd, for instance, was a member of both the Finance and Armed Services committees. Presumably he was in a position to apply a Senate standard regarding the conflict of interest issue as it affected each nomination. Yet he appeared to review Wilson's holdings differently from Humphrey's.

Wilson emerged from the hearings with his public reputation enhanced. Opinion polls showed that a majority of Americans felt that his previous experience in private industry would be an asset to him in the position. Although in Eisenhower's view he had made a substantial material sacrifice, he enthusiastically entered the administration and prepared to tackle the problems at the Pentagon.[33] His first encounter with official Washington had proved disappointing; nevertheless, Wilson was determined to make a positive impact on the nation's defense program. He certainly assumed his post at a crucial time. The Korean War was still in progress, the economy was shackled with wartime controls, and the defense budget had tripled during the previous three years. Dealing with these problems created additional controversy for Wilson as the administration attempted to tackle the defense budget for fiscal year 1954.

4

New Problems, Personalities, and Policies: Wilson and the Defense Department in 1953

W HEN Charles E. Wilson began to administer the Department of Defense in 1953, crucial military problems demanded his attention. Most important was the effective conduct of the war in Korea, a conflict stalemated on the battlefield but awaiting a successful breakthrough in negotiations between the Communist Chinese and Americans. Administrative difficulties at the Pentagon, arising from the need to reform certain inefficient and cumbersome wartime procedures, also required Wilson's time. Hanson Baldwin, military columnist for the *New York Times,* remarked that Wilson's primary managerial task should be to streamline the operations of the National Security Resources Board, an agency increasingly influential during the Korean War.[1]

In addition to the purely administrative functions of his office, Wilson faced a number of political decisions. One involved the selection of new Joint Chiefs of Staff to replace the group appointed during the Truman years. Senate Republicans, led by Robert Taft, wanted Eisenhower's commitment to nominate new military leaders whose views were more acceptable to the GOP than those of the supposedly European-oriented Truman staff. Wilson was to play a pivotal role in that selection as Eisenhower intended to strengthen the authority of the secretary of defense in the overall military picture. But Wilson's major political decision in 1953 occurred in early March, when he began his program to reduce some nonessential defense spending. Both the president and the secretary were concerned about the alarming rate of Pentagon expenditures and their effect on the civilian economy. Due to the requirements of the Korean War, the military budget had grown from $13 billion in 1949 to almost $47 billion in the 1954 fiscal year budget request which Truman submitted to Congress before leaving office.[2]

During the presidential campaign, Eisenhower had touched on his concern about excessive Pentagon spending. If elected, he stated, his administration would strive for a military program which gave both "security and solvency."[3] Eisenhower's views on budgetary restraint for defense squared with his other promises to reduce total government spending and work for a tax cut. Fulfilling those promises required substantial economizing at all levels of government, but chiefly at the Defense Department, where four-sevenths of all tax revenues were spent. But making those reductions hardly looked possible in 1953. The nation continued to fight in Korea, a fact which seemed to rule out any cutback in military spending. Yet Eisenhower and Wilson realized that, if reductions were to be achieved, a start toward that goal was necessary as soon as possible. When the new administration took office, Wilson instructed his defense planners to explore ways of reducing total expenditures without impairing the war effort or endangering national security.

Coupled with Wilson's achievements in the management of the Korean War effort, the administration's decision to submit an "interim" defense budget brought about a more efficient operation at the Pentagon during 1953. Nevertheless, the decision to reduce military spending during wartime was not a popular one. Democrats charged the Eisenhower administration, and Wilson in particular, with placing finances ahead of security. This administration, it was charged, preferred saving dollars to saving lives. Nor was the president's own party enthusiastic about the thrust of national defense policy under Wilson and Eisenhower. Some GOP moderates, such as Senator Homer Ferguson from Michigan, supported the administration consistently. But others, such as Taft, believed that the reductions which Eisenhower submitted were too small. In Taft's view, Charles E. Wilson was a considerable disappointment as secretary of defense, an official too willing to accept the military's recommendations.[4] From its beginning, it seemed that the administration was caught between its Democratic critics, who felt that more should be spent for defense, and suspicious Republicans who wanted more drastic reductions in federal spending.

Faced with this situation, the administration tried to steer a middle course in 1953. "The Eisenhower Shift," a military program designed to provide security for the nation at an affordable cost, began shortly after the new defense team assumed power. During his first year at the Pentagon, Charles Wilson became the visible and controversial spokesman for that policy, defending it before the Congress, the press, and the nation. He moved simultaneously on several fronts, keeping a close watch on the Korean situation while also looking for ways to improve the operation of the Pentagon and eliminate unnecessary expenses. Throughout 1953, the Pentagon was a place of intense activity, and one Washington reporter, after observing Wilson and his associates at work, remarked, "C.E. and his men are acting like they intend to be around for awhile."[5] His observation proved correct.

Wilson's first major problem in 1953 concerned the possibility of a severe shortage of ammunition for American troops in Korea. In testimony before a congressional committee, furloughed General James Van Fleet claimed that there was often not enough ammunition available for combat purposes. After Van Fleet's testimony, several influential senators expressed their concern and criticized the administration for failing to correct the situation. Harry Byrd, John McClellan, and Joseph McCarthy were the most outspoken on the issue.[6]

Van Fleet's allegations led to an inquiry into an alleged "Korean Shell Scandal." Not every military leader agreed with Van Fleet; some officers even issued public rebuttals of his testimony. General Omar Bradley, the chairman of the Joint Chiefs, General Mark Clark, the American commander in Korea, and Army Chief of Staff General J. Lawton Collins all gave statements assuring the public that American troops possessed sufficient ammunition. Wilson supported the army leadership and informally told Senate Armed Services Committee Chairman Saltonstall that no shell shortage existed. Nevertheless, Senate Majority Leader Taft called for an investigation of the Korean shell situation to resolve some of the contradictory statements. Wilson was asked to appear before the Armed Services Committee to explain the administration's position. In his testimony, the secretary contended that American troops in Korea had sufficient supplies of ammunition. Any past deficiencies had been corrected. Pointing out that he "visited Korea with President Eisenhower, General Bradley and others in early December," Wilson stated that he found no ammunition shortage. Furthermore, the secretary remarked that "while there I listened to discussions regarding the ammunition situation.... I questioned General Van Fleet regarding the enemy's rate of fire compared to our own."[7]

Wilson's remarks eased some of the confusion about the shell situation. The Armed Services Committee appointed a special subcommittee to investigate the various charges, which published a report of its findings in late May.[8] Maintaining that the shell shortage "resulted from a combination of errors and ineffective administration which involved practically everyone in whom responsibility has been invested," the document accepted Wilson's view that the shortage had been corrected. Curiously, Wilson was called upon to defend some administrative errors made before he became secretary of defense.

At any rate, Wilson intended to curtail that sort of administrative error. Before the shell situation diverted his attention, Wilson had begun work on a plan to reorganize the Defense Department. As a first step, he appointed a seven-member committee to study the possibility of effecting managerial reforms within the Pentagon bureaucracy.[9] This committee, informally referred to as "the Rockefeller Committee" after its chairman, Nelson Rockefeller, included David Sarnoff, president of the Radio Corporation of America, General Omar Bradley, Vannevar Bush, a prominent nuclear scientist, Chairman of the Office of Defense Mobilization Dr. Arthur Flemming, former secretary of defense Robert Lovett, and the president's brother, Dr. Milton Eisenhower. Later, Wilson appointed Admiral Chester Nimitz and General George C. Marshall as additional military consultants. Wilson entrusted this committee with the responsibility of submitting, within nine weeks, a plan for the reorganization of the Defense Department. The committee's recommendations would then be studied and formulated into a legislative proposal for congressional consideration.

Reorganization Plan 6, the product of the Rockefeller Committee, embodied three objectives which Eisenhower had wanted the committee to consider: strengthening civilian control over the military leadership; improving administrative procedures within the Defense Department; and making provisions for better strategic planning.[10] The outline of the committee's proposal recommended strengthening the position of secretary of defense and making better use of the latest technology in planning military strategy. Wilson used the committee's recommendations in formulating a proposal for congressional consideration, dividing the plan into its civilian and military parts in order to specify the type of operation he desired. As submitted to Congress, Plan 6 was a proposal for the reform of defense operations and an accurate picture of the way in which the Eisenhower administration conceived its military program.

The civilian-oriented aspects of the proposal included some of the suggestions which Baldwin had made in the *New York Times,* reforms designed to improve defense planning. For instance, Wilson planned to abolish the complex of agencies which Truman had installed to administer the Korean War. Under Plan 6, the secretary intended to dismantle the Munitions Board, the Research and Development Board, the Defense Supply Management Agency, and the Director of Installations. He asked for the authority to appoint six additional assistant secretaries of defense who would report to him regarding administrative problems involved in these defense operations. The six areas would be research and development; applications engineering; supply and logistics; properties and installations; legislative and public affairs; and health and medical affairs. Wilson had inherited an administrative structure which included assistant secretaries for international affairs, manpower and personnel, and finance; these additional posts would bring the number of assistant secretaries to nine.[11] Furthermore, he requested a general counsel who would represent the Pentagon in legal matters and serve as an equal to the assistant secretaries. Through these recommendations, Wilson hoped to complete the civilian reorganization of the Pentagon.[12]

Plan 6 also contained two important provisions pertaining to military affairs. First, it recommended that the secretary of defense select the chairman of the Joint Chiefs of Staff, thereby making him more directly responsible to the civilian leadership. But it also recommended that the chairman participate more fully in political-military decision making as the defense secretary's principal military adviser.[13]

Wilson submitted Plan 6 to Congress in late April. The Government Operations Committee of the House of Representatives, which initially reviewed the plan, expressed general approval of the civilian reorganization provisions. But the military provisions which enlarged the authority of the chairman of the Joint Chiefs of Staff encountered some opposition. The committee's basic complaint about this proposal was that it provided the Army with an inordinate amount of power in the military command. At the time, two Army men were members of the Joint Chiefs—the chairman, General Omar Bradley, and Army Chief of Staff General J. Lawton Collins. In addition, Eisenhower, a former general, was now commander-in-chief of the military establishment. During the hearings on Reorganization Plan 6, the Army's service rivals charged that the administration was trying to construct a "Prussianized General Staff" reminiscent of the army-dominated general staff of Weimar Germany in the years immediately following World War I. Brigadier General Robert Johnson, chairman of the board of directors of Johnson and Johnson Corporation, argued that point clearly in the hearings. Johnson, a prominent leader in the National Guard, told the Government Operations Committee that the army general staff was "engaged in an unrelenting struggle for power."[14] The concern over possible abuses of the Army's power under the plan served temporarily to stall its approval in the House.

Plan 6 was considered by the entire House in late June. Still outstanding was the fear of a "Prussian single staff," a fear which increased the possibility that the bill might be amended in a way unacceptable to the administration. Administration aides therefore went to work in the House, attempting to defuse opposition. After several days of maneuvering, the House approved the plan on 27 June. The Senate took no action on the bill, and it went into effect on 29 June.[15] With its passage, Wilson received the authority to administer the Pentagon according to his preferences and desires.

Wilson was pleased with the congressional approval of Pentagon reorganization. Plan 6 permitted him to organize the Defense Department more like a corporate management structure. Indeed, the assistant secretaries corresponded to the various vice-presidents in the General Motors scheme; they had planning, advisory, and executive responsibilities. The secretary on several occasions even referred to them as "my vice-presidents."[16] Although corporate bureaucracies may be as clumsy as other bureaucracies, Wilson placed tremendous confidence in the General Motors management structure as a model for providing clarity, efficiency, and authority to complex organizations. Plan 6 was useful to the extent that it made the Pentagon leadership comfortable in determining future operations. Two years later, however, one Washington analyst wrote that the adoption of Plan 6 had allowed Wilson to reduce 160,000 jobs throughout the Defense Department at a savings of almost $900 million. H. Struve Hensel, Wilson's first general counsel, also wrote in early 1954 that "the replacement of the Munitions Board by an Assistant Secretary for Supply and Logistics has resulted in the reduction of staff personnel in that area (exclusive of cataloguing activities) from 449 as of January, 1953, to 232 as of October, 1953."[17]

That Eisenhower had no specific intention of using the Reorganization Plan 6 as a means of elevating the Army's role in military affairs became evident in mid-May, when the administration announced its wish to appoint new members of the Joint Chiefs of Staff. Had Eisenhower appointed an Army officer to replace Bradley as chairman, there might have been cause for concern, but the president had already decided that Navy Admiral Arthur Radford would be the next chairman. However, the selection of a new group of military advisers did present some political problems for the administration. Senator Taft and other members of the Republican right wanted new service chieftains who would champion the GOP's traditional interest in Pacific affairs. General Bradley, as well as Truman's other military advisers, had supported former Secretary of State Acheson's European-oriented foreign policy. In so doing, Bradley and the other Joint Chiefs had alienated the Republican leadership.

When Eisenhower kept his campaign pledge and visited Korea in December 1952, Wilson, Dulles, Humphrey, and several other key advisers accompanied him. On the return trip, Wilson met with Admiral Radford in Hawaii to determine his suitability for the chairmanship of the Joint Chiefs. Radford certainly possessed the credentials necessary to satisfy the GOP's conservative element. A strong believer in air power, he had earned a reputation as a tough, resolute naval commander. During campaigns against the Japanese in World War II, he advocated "killing the bastards scientifically." Furthermore, Radford spoke of a "positive" policy toward Nationalist China, which in the terminology of the Republican right wing meant "unleashing Chiang Kai-Shek" for the possible "liberation" of mainland China. Radford's military and political views were certainly satisfactory to a restive segment of the party whose support Eisenhower needed for future defense matters.[18]

Eisenhower and Wilson did more than merely satisfy a party faction by examining Radford for the nation's top military position. At the time, the admiral held the title of Commander-in-Chief, Pacific (CINCPAC) and articulated the military philosophy favored by Eisenhower, Wilson, and Treasury Secretary Humphrey. While Eisenhower and Wilson later served to counter Radford's more hawkish tendencies, the admiral promised to be useful as a congressional lobbyist for the administration's future defense policy. Radford was forceful, persuasive, and committed to the new strategic military technology.[19] Impressed with Radford, Wilson passed along a favorable report about him to Eisenhower. It was thus understood that Radford would become chairman of the Joint Chiefs of Staff when Bradley resigned in 1953. Some doubts lingered about Radford's potential as a member of the Eisenhower team because of his part in the "Admirals' Revolt" against Secretary of Defense Johnson's leadership in 1949.[20] But the administration decided to overlook those doubts and stay with Radford, who said his views had changed about that action anyway. His selection served two important purposes: it guaranteed a military chief who met the president's criteria in military thinking; and it also satisfied a suspicious party faction whose support was essential in the months ahead.

But the selection of the other service chiefs had not been agreed upon prior to Eisenhower's inauguration. Thus, in early April, Eisenhower and Wilson began a formal consideration of other possible military leaders to head the various service branches. On 12 May, the administration formally announced the selection of a new Joint Chiefs of Staff which would serve on a stand-by basis until the term of the current members expired 15 August. The administration's first Joint Chiefs included Chairman Admiral Radford, Army Chief of Staff General Matthew B. Ridgway, Chief of Naval Operations Admiral Robert Carney, and Chief of Staff for the Air Force General Nathan F. Twining. The new Joint Chiefs were experienced military leaders, men who had seen previous service in both the European and Pacific commands.

Taft later denied that he had personally chosen the Joint Chiefs but did confirm that he played a leading part in the selection process. Before the administration announced its choices, Wilson invited the senator to his suite at Wardman Park Hotel to consider the nominees. Over scotch and soda, the men conferred about the political acceptability of the prospective choices. "Wilson had me to his apartment," Taft recalled, "and showed me the list. I found it entirely satisfactory."[21] So while Wilson and Eisenhower bent somewhat to Taft's preferences on the matter, their action allowed them to have a military leadership of their choosing and also keep the most powerful Senate Republican on their side for the upcoming debate over the fate of the Pentagon budget.

Wilson's performance in the first four months of 1953 demonstrated his intention to take a leading role in the implementation of military policy. The secretary had shown an ability to manage the war effort and also tend to the political functions of his office. Yet his achievements in the first few months of 1953, such as the reorganization of the Defense Department, were less important to the overall success of the administration's defense policy than his efforts to trim nonessential spending from the Pentagon budget. Formulating the so-called interim budget occupied most of the late spring and summer and brought the administration to a major test of strength with the political opposition. It also produced differences of opinion with several influential military leaders.

President Eisenhower's approach to defense policy was consistent with his general view of economic affairs. Both philosophically and politically, the administration was committed to the goal of a balanced federal budget. Defense spending accounted for more than half the total of federal expenditures in the early 1950s, and if the administration expected to achieve any overall reduction, military spending would not be exempt from some trimming. Eisenhower did not decide to reduce Pentagon expenditures out of any pique at the military, but out of a commitment to restrain what he felt was a dangerous

trend in government economic policy. One could argue with his decision, yet it is important to realize that the administration sought economy in every area, not simply defense.

While it might have been desirable to reduce some nonessential
military expenditures, international and domestic political conditions
in 1953 seriously militated against such a course of action. The nation
was fighting a war in Korea, and Soviet intentions in the world arena
were suspect. Reducing one's military capability at such a time hardly
appeared wise. But by the first of August, the administration had
scored a series of noteworthy triumphs. First, the war in Korea
ground to an uneasy truce in late July, and American prisoners of war
soon returned home. At the Pentagon, Wilson presided over a $5
billion reduction in military expenditures made possible chiefly
through better management, revised strategic planning, and more
efficient procedures. Most important, the secretary made these
economies without impairing the war effort. Furthermore, he designed these measures in the hope that defense policy would be on a
firmer foundation for the next several years and that long-range
planning could replace an emphasis on the military establishment's
immediate problems.

However, that $5 billion reduction also bore a political price tag.
From the beginning of Wilson's economy efforts in early March until
the adoption of the interim budget in August, Senate Democrats
charged that the administration sacrificed security for dollars, and
that the secretary browbeat the services into compliance with his so-
called economy drive. Promilitary columnists, such as Joseph and
Stewart Alsop, reinforced Democratic charges and urged the administration to spend more on defense.[22] And the military, after receiving
large increases in funding because of the Korean War, expressed its
reluctance to accept a partial demobilization and return to the relatively lean periods usually occurring in peacetime. The military's hostility to Wilson's proposed reductions also entered into the political
equation in 1953.

Before examining the specific details of Wilson's administrative and
political decision, one should explore his rationale for making reductions. Wilson simply believed that the Pentagon budget was vastly
inflated. Past experience in industry had taught him that virtually

every organization contained some waste. Thus, a capable manager could make reductions in that waste while improving and strengthening the entire operation. In 1953, as in later years, Wilson proposed to reduce unnecessary Pentagon spending through a combination of improved administrative measures and revisions of strategic goals and force levels. He believed that his efforts would serve to upgrade and modernize the military's performance while also maintaining sufficient strategic capability.

In early February, Wilson began a review of the entire Pentagon operation in an effort to find areas where economies might be achieved. Indeed, every government department conducted such a review at the request of Budget Director Joseph Dodge.[23] Wilson spent most of February making this review, and by the end of the month, expressed his views on the matter to Congress. On 24 February, appearing before the House Appropriations Committee to explain the administration's defense program, he discussed his belief in the necessity for budget cuts.

> Our approach is based on the belief that we are all devoted to the task of achieving adequate security for our country at minimum cost. I am sure that none of us wish to spend one unnecessary dollar of tax money, but at the same time we must not lose sight of the responsibility regarding the safety of our nation.[24]

He also mentioned some possible ways of economizing on the defense budget, including savings brought about by the Pentagon reorganization, savings made through the adoption of practices recommended by the Rockefeller Committee, and savings achieved by reducing "lead time" through a better appraisal of defense contracting.[25]

Wilson's testimony before the Appropriations Committee showed that the administration intended to make some savings on defense, but he did not specify exactly which areas could expect reductions. In that sense, the secretary's statements were not controversial since he failed to single out any one program which would be curtailed. The real controversy developed in early March, when Wilson began to detail the nature of the reductions.

In March, Wilson's ax fell on some of the less essential Pentagon expenditures. On 12 March, he ordered the armed services to eliminate 39,346 civilian jobs by the end of May, and he also instructed the military to reduce its number of desk jobs. Those reductions, Wilson argued, would save the government $132 million.[26] One week after announcing these reductions. Wilson held a news conference at which he answered questions dealing with the curtailment and its impact on the political scene. One reporter asked the secretary if he was concerned about the criticism made by Senators Johnson and Symington about his policies. Wilson replied: "People will have honest disagreements, but I don't think any of us should lay awake nights for fear we are going to be blasted into eternity tomorrow morning."[27] Thinking that a $4–5 billion reduction in Pentagon expenditures was possible, the secretary indicated his intention to reduce the stockpile of wartime materials and refuse to purchase any nonessential supplies.

Wilson neglected to mention any cutbacks or readjustments in appropriations for the armed services branches, mainly because the administration had not yet decided on the extent of those reductions. But those reductions were soon to come. On 23 March, the *Wall Street Journal* speculated that Wilson had decided that the Navy and Air Force budgets offered the best opportunities for economies. Because of the hostilities in Korea, the Army would probably maintain its present level of funding.

After hammering out the details of the interim budget in April, the administration presented its revised defense estimates to Congress in early May. Eisenhower's budget reduced the Truman requests by almost $5 billion, from $40.7 billion to $35.8 billion. The Army received a slight increase in its funding, but the Navy and Air Force sustained losses. The Air Force budget was significantly curtailed; almost $5 billion was cut from the amount which Truman had originally requested. The Navy could hardly be pleased with the administration's proposal either; its appropriation was reduced by $1.7 billion.[28]

Wilson defended this revised Pentagon budget in a number of press conferences and congressional appearances during May and early June. On 11 May, Wilson testified before a House Appropriations Committee subcommittee and defended the administration's action, pointing out that national security required a substantial appropriation for defense, but that the administration wanted security with solvency.[29] An especially crucial item in Wilson's plans involved the concept of a sound mobilization base. The secretary wished to improve the Defense Department's production and procurement programs so that deliveries of materials would be in line with the administration's strategic goals. One of Wilson's primary tasks involved coordinating the supply and management programs in order to reduce lead time in the various areas of defense planning and procurement. By placing defense contracts with industries possessing the necessary technology, he hoped to reduce lead time and exert greater discipline on the Pentagon's procurement effort.

Wilson intended to streamline the mobilization base through improved coordination between the Pentagon and its contractors. He also wanted the armed services to move ahead with the development of their reserve programs so that, in the post-Korea period, the nation could reduce its number of uniformed personnel. But the secretary's decisions created problems for both the military and the nation's legislators. Congressmen and senators often used their acquisition of lucrative defense contracts for industries in their home districts as proof of their political effectiveness. Wilson proposed not only a reduction in total defense expenditures but also the awarding of defense contracts according to ability to produce, rather than on purely political grounds. For its part, the military knew that men in uniform meant dollars in the services' pockets. A reserve program would be attractive to any administration which wanted to cut expenditures but not to military leaders who hoped to keep funding at a comfortable level. Furthermore, increased interservice feuding became a distinct possibility if Wilson cut expenditures. With less money available, the services could be expected to compete even more strenuously for their respective shares.

Nevertheless, Wilson continued to push ahead with his defense of the interim budget. After his 11 May testimony on Capitol Hill, he held a press conference to discuss the apprehension developing in response to the budget cuts. Press questions centered specifically on the cuts in the Air Force budget and an item relating to the mobilization base, a 16 percent reduction for funds involving research and development.

Truman and his military planners had envisioned an Air Force with a deployment capability of 143 wings by fiscal year 1955. A wing—a group of aircraft available for a specific strategic purpose—contained no specific number of planes, but usually included bombers, interceptors, tactical support fighters, and cargo planes. Eisenhower and Wilson revised Truman's estimates from 143 to 120 wings, with an eventual goal of 137.[30] Wilson defended the reduction by citing some production statistics to clarify the status of the service. The 120-wing goal was an acceptable option, the secretary explained, because the Air Force had been receiving money and letting contracts far in advance of the actual delivery of planes. Furthermore, the service received some planes when it lacked the personnel either to fly or maintain them. As a result, the administration faced the possibility of having a number of "paper wings," planes which existed only in the planning stages.[31]

Wilson also commented on the 16 percent reduction in research and development funds. "R and D," the area where new technological and scientific innovations were explored, was a particularly glamorous part of the defense budget. But in Wilson's view, it was also an area of considerable waste.

> It is very easy to waste money in what you call research, that is, people hide behind the name and go ahead with a lot of boondoggling. You have to have really well-directed projects to avoid wasting money . . . and it is true on industrial research for commercial purposes or any kind of thing. It is just a question of getting that organized and controlled like anything else. Just because somebody calls it research, don't think it's wonderful.[32]

Wilson's attitude toward the benefits to be gained from defense research became particularly controversial. As was consistent with his previous experience in industry, Wilson believed that a goal of any research project was to shorten, as much as possible, the length of time between planning and implementation. Many of the secretary's critics, including some of Eisenhower's scientific advisers, faulted Wilson for his reluctance to take a more long-term approach to research and development activities. However, the Defense Department did make striking technological advances in the development of weapons systems between 1953 and 1957. Wilson understood the importance of research and development, but he insisted that any project meet the administration's criteria, which was sometimes unsatisfactory to those who believed that a greater effort was necessary in this area.[33]

On 15 May the secretary of defense spoke at the Armed Services Day Dinner in Washington, using the occasion to summarize the current status of the Pentagon's operation and to offer some thoughts about future policy. Admittedly, the Eisenhower administration had proposed some strong medicine for the military services. But Wilson contended that these steps were necessary to reach its objective, a more efficient and less cumbersome national defense operation.

> I see no reason to stockpile such items as typewriters, adding machines, paint, lumber, pencils, brooms, toilet paper, furniture, standard trucks and passenger cars as part of the mobilization reserve. . . .
>
> Our economy program, and we do have an economy program, is based on more effective defense for less money. We believe that Uncle Sam's big old pocketbook has been open just too wide. Crash programs and easy spending can no longer be justified, if they ever could. It is reasonable to expect the Defense Department to spend the money available to it in the same frugal, objective way that the people themselves have to spend what money they have left over after they pay their big taxes.[34]

After Wilson's week of meetings, press conferences, and speeches, Eisenhower met with key congressional leaders between 19 and 21 May to lend his support to the interim budget. The president reinforced Wilson's earlier statements about the cuts in the Air Force budget. Warning against the economic dangers involved in playing a "numbers game," Eisenhower voiced his distrust of "paper wings." Neither the military nor the nation could achieve absolute security; a better objective was realistic force levels based on economic and political, as well as military, considerations. But when Congress began its consideration of the interim budget, an immediate outcry arose in protest of the reductions in the Air Force budget. Democratic Representative Sam Yorty from California, a state which had a significant economic stake in the aircraft industry, was especially critical of Secretary Wilson, saying angrily: "The threat to our national security inherent in Secretary Wilson's pennywise assault on our Air Force is too serious to warrant his retention at the head of the Defense Department. Wilson is a defeatist Secretary whose vision is so circumscribed by dollars, profits and grossly exaggerated economic strain that he is willing to concede Russia indefinite superiority in the air."[35]

In the Senate, Wilson's proposed reductions met considerable opposition from Democrats, while Republicans muted their skepticism in deference to Eisenhower's military judgment. Some Republican moderates, such as Michigan's Homer Ferguson, who sat on the Armed Services Committee, supported the administration's position. But Wilson's occasional critic, Lyndon B. Johnson, sarcastically remarked that, in the secretary's logic, "fewer ships, fewer guns and fewer planes mean greater strength."[36] By the beginning of June, Congress prepared for a full-dress review of the interim budget with the participation of both the civilian and military leadership.

The military leaders' concern over budget reductions brought about their first open break with Wilson. On 5 June, General Hoyt Vandenberg, the outgoing air force chief of staff, testified to a Senate Appropriations Committee subcommittee that the revised Air Force budget allocated too little money to guarantee that the service could "resist a Communist attack." His remarks differed sharply with Wilson's previous statements; the secretary had maintained that the Air Force budget was designed for a defensive purpose. Vandenberg sought to convince the subcommittee of the necessity for a greater appropriation for the Air Force, arguing that the service needed to reach its previous target of 143 wings by the end of 1955 or face the possibility of falling drastically behind the Soviet Union in overall air strength. Vandenberg stated that "the Soviet Air Force has both offensive and defensive capability," with the clear implication that American air power was only defensive. Furthermore, he contended that the civilian leadership—Eisenhower, Wilson, and Secretary of the Treasury Humphrey—had excluded the Joint Chiefs from participating in the decision to lower the target from 143 wings to 120. Vandenberg clearly believed that the administration had scaled back its strategic capability solely to fulfill its pledge of balancing the federal budget by reducing military expenditures.[37]

Vandenberg's testimony placed the administration in a difficult position, at least temporarily. Certainly no responsible leader wanted to

THERE'S NO SUCH THING AS A PERFECT DEFENSE

By permission of *The Washington Star*

imperil national security by drastically reducing military strength. So Wilson, privately very angry over Vandenberg's remarks, again journeyed to Capitol Hill to present the administration's case for the reductions.[38] On 8 June, the secretary spoke to a subcommittee of the Senate Appropriations Committee. He explained that while the Air Force was sustaining some monetary cutbacks, the administration did not intend to sacrifice overall air capability. Pointing out that both the Army and Navy possessed air components, Wilson instructed the senators to consider that fact when they reviewed the nation's total air strength. Wilson also contended that Vandenberg's charge that the administration excluded the Joint Chiefs was false. They were consulted, the secretary stated, but they were instructed to submit estimates of the levels of strength which could be maintained without a tax increase. Economic and political factors did enter into the military picture, Wilson stated; it was naive to assume otherwise. He assured the senators: "Most emphatically we are not going to have the second-best Air Force."[39]

The highlight of Wilson's testimony to the committee occurred when he dealt with the criticisms voiced by military leaders about the interim budget. General Curtis LeMay, the commander of the Strategic Air Command, had joined Vandenberg in insisting that Wilson's proposals posed "unacceptable risks" to American security. The secretary defended his decisions:

> I sense from some of the statements of military leaders a desire to build up such forces as could defend the whole world. This is simply beyond our capability over the long run. We have provided tremendous grants to allied nations in order to get them in a position so they could defend themselves and thus contribute substantially to the overall ground, air and naval strength of the free world. These plans are now coming into fruition.

He pointed out that his main intention was to eliminate "extravagance and waste." Using the argument that national security was endangered in order to receive a greater appropriation was, in the secretary's words, an "old military trick." Wilson mentioned that he would "like to see Curt LeMay have a real nice, good set up out there, but he is getting along pretty well."[40]

The Appropriations Committee subcommittee apparently chose to believe the secretary of defense instead of the Air Force chieftains. In their report, the senators stated that a number of considerations entered into any decision made about military spending. On the one hand, the survival of the free world required an acceptable level of national defense. But on the other, that military buildup could not be so great as to bring about a regimentation of civilian life. Nevertheless, a minority of the subcommittee continued to speak out against Wilson's policy. Several prominent Democrats, and Republican maverick Wayne Morse, continued their campaign against the revised defense program.

By permission of *The Washington Star*

Stuart Symington, a leading proponent of increased air power, led the Democratic attacks against the cuts in Air Force spending. The senator from Missouri, less concerned than the administration about the cost of national defense, argued: "As far as the civilian economy is concerned, whatever is necessary to maintain the 143 group program should be allocated." Other Democrats, not convinced of the soundness of Wilson's or Eisenhower's military judgment, joined Symington. Hubert H. Humphrey, a freshman Democrat from Minnesota, observed:

What we need in Congress is not merely to remember the mistakes of history, but to profit from those mistakes. . . . I believe that the burden of proof rests upon the administration to show that the masters of the Soviet Union have dropped their features of vultures and taken on the features of a dove. . . . I do not want to listen to Mr. Wilson, who believes he must keep a campaign promise to cut the budget without regard for the facts of the international situation.

In similar fashion, Senator Morse charged the administration with submitting a defense budget which was "against the best interests of the American people." Morse was especially critical of Eisenhower, whom he considered "not a good expert" on military reality.

I do not turn to Mr. Eisenhower for the best expert testimony on defense needs and the defense budget. Neither do I turn to Mr. Wilson. I do not believe that either man is the best qualified man in the country to tell the American people what the defense budget ought to be.

I prefer to accept the testimony of those who have warned us time and time again of the seriousness of the situation confronting us. . . . such witnesses as General Vandenberg.[41]

After the June speeches, arguments, and counterarguments, the Senate began its formal consideration of the interim budget in early July. On 2 July, the president sent a message to Congress emphasizing the injurious effect which a defense budget that sought total military protection might have on the economy. Referring to Vandenberg and LeMay, Eisenhower warned against "the ever-present struggle of service partisans for larger proportions of the defense dollar."[42] Fortunately for the administration, the Republicans controlled Congress, and many GOP legislators were even more economy-minded than Wilson. The debate over the budget lasted until 29 July, when both houses approved a final package totaling $34.4 billion, almost $1.5 billion less than the administration originally requested. Two amendments to add almost $500 million to the Air Force budget, proposed by Democratic Senators Carl Hayden of Arizona and Burnett Maybank of South Carolina, were defeated on virtual party-line votes. Thus H.R. 5969, the Eisenhower administration's interim budget, passed its congressional test and became law when the president signed it on 1 August.[43]

Admiral Arthur Radford, chairman of the Joint Chiefs of Staff, was Wilson's primary military adviser. This photograph was taken in February 1955, when the two men appeared before a House subcommittee to testify in support of a pay raise for the military.

Wilson at the U.S. Air Force base in Frankfurt, Germany, on 15 April 1953. He was on an official tour of U.S. defense installations in West Germany, but he also took the opportunity to confer with General Matthew Ridgway, who was under consideration for Army chief of staff. From left to right: Wilson; Ridgway; Secretary of the Army Robert T. Stevens; General Thomas T. Handy. Visible in the back is Vice-admiral Jerauld Wright.

If the Korean situation had worsened during 1953, Eisenhower and Wilson would have been even more severely criticized for reductions in Pentagon spending. But the deadlocked negotiations at Panmunjom broke in late July, and the conflict reached an uneasy truce. Thus, in a modified way, Eisenhower kept two campaign promises in 1953: his administration managed to settle the war and make reductions in federal spending. Considering the times and the political opposition to those policies, even these limited triumphs were no small accomplishment. Wilson was understandably proud of the progress which the Defense Department made under his direction in 1953. The secretary contributed a brief article to *Nation's Business* in January 1954, where he outlined the success of the previous year. He wrote:

> In the first year of the present Administration, we have seen the end of the fighting in Korea, the return of American war prisoners to their homes, the reorganization of the Department of Defense, the orderly reduction of $5.3 billion from the defense budget submitted by the previous Administration and the emergence of a realistic defense program.
>
> The objective of the entire defense organization is to develop the maximum military strength and security that can be obtained for our country by the intelligent expenditures of funds that the people of our country are able and willing through the Congress to make available for defense purposes.[44]

Although the achievements were considerable, Wilson paid a political price for them. In the eyes of the Democratic opposition, he remained the penny-pinching businessman-bureaucrat, more concerned with dollars than lives. The military leadership, too, came to realize that Wilson intended to examine their future appropriations more carefully than had been true in the previous three or four years. Vandenberg's criticism of the secretary's reductions in the Air Force budget signaled the opening round of the military's campaign to prevent Wilson from curtailing military funding. But Wilson was committed to a defense program which included careful cost analysis as a significant element in military programming. The planning for Eisenhower's first defense budget began in the last few months of 1953 and occupied most of Wilson's attention during that time. Beginning in 1954, however, a new problem in the Senate came to plague the secretary and the entire military establishment. With the anti-Communist hysteria surging throughout the nation, Wilson was called to defend his department and its procedures against the attacks of the junior senator from Wisconsin, Joseph R. McCarthy.

5

Combating Hysteria: The Internal Security Issue

FOR Charles E. Wilson, 1954 was a tumultuous year. The Eisenhower administration presented its first military budget, a program called "the New Look," which was designed to provide greater security for the nation at much less cost than previous defense spending. It fell to Wilson, as secretary of defense, to guide the New Look through a hostile and skeptical Congress. That task would have constituted a full year's worth of effort, but other events interrupted Wilson and diverted his attention from his more immediate responsibilities. Specifically, 1954 was the year when Joseph R. McCarthy, the Republican junior senator from Wisconsin from 1946 to 1957, attempted to investigate the Pentagon, alleging that the Defense Department contained Communist subversives. McCarthy's attacks on federal departments, made in the name of exposing Communists, Communist sympathizers, and "fellow travelers," occupied national attention during the early 1950s and won him a national reputation and following.[1]

McCarthy directed his anti-Communist investigations primarily against the State Department and the various national security agencies which emerged during the postwar period. During the Truman years, the senator maligned both George C. Marshall and Dean Acheson, the president's two respected secretaries of state. In McCarthy's view, Acheson was one of those officials responsible for "losing" China to the Communists.[2] In similar fashion, McCarthy once characterized Marshall as part of a worldwide Communist conspiracy.[3] Between 1950 and the time Eisenhower took office in January 1953, McCarthy had also included the Voice of America and the Central Intelligence Agency in his accusations. The Democratic party left power in 1953 after being savaged for two years by the senator's charges.

Despite the ferocity of his attacks, McCarthy was only a part of what became known as "McCarthyism." As Truman told Merle Miller during a series of interviews in 1962, "the ones who encouraged McCarthy were just as bad." Said the peppery former president:

... of course, it wasn't just McCarthy. A fella like that couldn't have gotten anywhere if he'd been fought from the very beginning. . . . People like Taft [Senator Robert A. Taft . . .], he knew that what McCarthy was saying wasn't true, that he was demagoguing the issue for all it was worth, and he knew that was a dangerous thing to do. . . . But he said, you know, that if McCarthy didn't have the facts in one case, he should keep on making accusations until he got to one where he could come up with the facts.

Now that's where the real danger comes; it isn't only the demagogues. It's the ones who encourage them, who'll do anything in the world to win an election. They're just as bad.[4]

Truman mentioned Taft as one prominent Republican who embraced McCarthyism, and in truth, much of the Republican right jumped on the senator's wagon and helped create the problem Eisenhower faced when he came to power in 1953. As a moderate, the president did not share McCarthy's views about so-called Communists in government. But he faced the necessity of keeping the party in order and not increasing the suspicion which many conservative members of the GOP felt about his presidency. Furthermore, no one was certain what Eisenhower's victory meant to the future of McCarthyism. Liberal Republicans, such as Emmett John Hughes, hoped that Eisenhower would use his influence as party leader to neutralize the Wisconsin senator.[5] Many conservative Republicans, however, considered their elections in 1952 as a resounding mandate for continued investigations into subversive infiltration of the government. Vice-president Richard M. Nixon, a prominent voice among party conservatives, had vowed during the campaign "to drive the crooks and the Communists out of Washington." His presence on the Republican ticket had signified a legitimizing of McCarthyism to the vocal anti-Communist element of the GOP.[6]

Faced with this uncertain situation, Eisenhower temporized and refused to break with McCarthy. Such indecision soon reflected itself in cabinet affairs, the area of Wilson's responsibility. Secretary of State John Foster Dulles, the most influential member of the cabinet, began his tenure with a rhetoric designed to keep the troops on the right content. Speaking to a group of State Department employees on the day after Eisenhower's inauguration, he warned that not "competence and discipline," but "positive loyalty" would be the test of a capable foreign service official. Anything less was "not tolerable." Over the next several months, Dulles accelerated the decline in morale at the State Department. At McCarthy's insistence, he allowed a right-wing former FBI agent named Scott McLeod to examine the department's security files for possible "subversives." Dulles dismissed such brilliant foreign policy thinkers as John Carter Vincent, John Paton Davies, and George Kennan for making "administrative errors."[7] To a department already reeling from half a decade of partisan attack, Dulles's suspicions of disloyalty were especially unwelcome.

Wilson and the Department of Defense encountered no difficulty with McCarthy during 1953. But in 1954, the secretary was called to deal with several events which brought the integrity of the department and its internal security procedures into question. Throughout the year, the secretary of defense was required to testify on the Pentagon's policy regarding security risks, to initiate new loyalty reviews, and to defend the record of his subordinates who were being investigated by McCarthy. Although the early years of the Eisenhower administration were marked by a tendency toward repression and acceptance of McCarthy's charges, with no appreciable concern for the constitutional rights of individuals who were the objects of his attacks, Wilson neither joined the McCarthy witch-hunt nor approved of the senator's tactics.

Wilson's approach to the anti-Communist issue contrasted with that of Dulles on at least two levels. First, Wilson submitted proposals to Congress when he decided that changes in internal security policy were necessary. He did not conduct his own loyalty review independently of the other branches of government. Second, he required the armed services to implement their own security reviews, complete with appeals for anyone presumed subversive. Furthermore, he instructed the services to make their reports public and state concretely their estimate of any internal security problem. Uppermost in Wilson's mind was the need to develop a system which specified the difference between a "subversive," a "loyalty risk," and the other categories invented by the senator from Wisconsin. Wilson persisted in the belief that McCarthy's charges against any Defense Department employee could be proven false if the senator would state specifically the nature of his accusation.

It was evident throughout 1954 that Wilson was both annoyed and angered by McCarthy's antics. Just prior to the opening of the Army-McCarthy Hearings in the spring of 1954, when the McCarthy hysteria was at its crest, Wilson remarked that the senator's charges that "the Army was coddling Communists was just damn tommyrot." He also spoke of his concern for constitutional abuses which might result from McCarthyism, as in a speech to the national convention of the U.S. Chamber of Commerce on 26 April 1954: "Time does not permit me to dwell on the importance of maintaining our free institutions and our respect for individual human rights. In our efforts to eliminate subversives and security risks, we must avoid using the methods of a tyrant."[8] Nor did Wilson countenance outside criticism of his appointees. He trusted his subordinates and defended them in several speeches and press conferences. To the best of my knowledge, no Defense Department employee was ever asked to resign because of charges made against him by McCarthy. Mindful of the necessity of good morale in any successful organization, Wilson attempted to sustain it through his public utterances.

Nevertheless, the Pentagon bureaucracy and even the armed services were under attack by McCarthy throughout 1954. In order to allay any public suspicion that the military establishment was influenced by Communist subversives, Wilson had to deal with four extremely sensitive problems. One was the investigation of charges that Dr. J. Robert Oppenheimer, the nuclear physicist, was a security risk because of his past associations with Communists. Another was the need to amend the statute dealing with the induction of physicians into the armed services. A third was the need for a constitutional review of the policies the Defense Department used in determining criteria for identifying disloyal employees or security risks. The fourth problem, and the most thorny one, was monitoring the Army's position in the celebrated Army-McCarthy Hearings. Wilson's administrative performance on the internal security issues contained some errors, as did those of most administration officials who dealt with McCarthy. Yet his behavior was certainly respectable by comparison with those Republicans who totally embraced the senator's cause and tactics.

Wilson's introduction to the loyalty issue occurred in late 1953, when he was called upon to investigate charges that Oppenheimer might be disloyal. On 7 November 1953, a young lawyer named William L. Borden sent two letters, one to the chairman of the Joint Congressional Committee on Atomic Energy and another to the director of the FBI, alleging that "J. Robert Oppenheimer was, more probably than not, an agent of the Soviet Union." Borden, who had previously served as executive secretary of the Joint Congressional Committee on Atomic Energy during the Truman administration, outlined Oppenheimer's early opposition to the development of the hydrogen bomb and his pre-World War II friendships with known Communists. J. Edgar Hoover, the director of the FBI, then ordered a summary of Oppenheimer's security file and directed that it be sent to the White House and to the secretary of defense.[9]

Wilson spoke with Eisenhower on 2 December, fearful that if McCarthy learned the contents of the letter he would use them to smear both Oppenheimer and the administration. The administration faced a difficult political and moral decision. Were the charges against the physicist sufficient to warrant his dismissal from the government? At the time, Oppenheimer served occasionally as a consultant to the Atomic Energy Commission, which had requested his advice only twice since 1953. He had resigned as chairman of the Government Advisory Committee on Atomic Energy before Eisenhower's election. Thus he was not as active in the government's nuclear research as he had been in the late 1940s.

The contents of Borden's letter shocked Eisenhower and Wilson. Hoover had known of Oppenheimer's pre-World War II associations with Communists on the West Coast and of his friendship with a

French Communist, Haakon Chevalier. Borden's allegation that Oppenheimer sought to impede progress on research for the hydrogen bomb was, however, the charge which most concerned the administration. Lewis Strauss, the chairman of the Atomic Energy Commission, verified the physicist's opposition to the development of the weapon, claiming that he was aware of Oppenheimer's attitude as early as 1947.[10]

On 3 December, Wilson met at the White House with the president, Strauss, National Security Assistant Robert Cutler, Attorney General Herbert Brownell, and Dr. Arthur Flemming, director of the Office of Defense Mobilization. At that meeting, the officials discussed the painful options available in the Oppenheimer matter. Eisenhower narrowed the choices to three: asking for a formal hearing on the charges against the scientist; discreetly requesting and accepting Oppenheimer's resignation; or simply allowing the physicist's consulting contract to lapse, as it would in June, without further requesting his services.[11] The second and third options presented the most humane ways of dealing with Oppenheimer, whose work had done much to strengthen America militarily. But those two choices posed some obvious political risks, especially if McCarthy learned of the contents of Borden's letters. If Oppenheimer simply resigned, possibly McCarthy would attack the administration for not dealing punitively with him. If he remained on the government payroll and McCarthy were to find out, the administration would be liable to charges that it was harboring a known Communist. Wilson stated that the officials should make a decision on the proper course before McCarthy or his staff became aware of the investigation.[12]

Eisenhower directed Strauss to begin a review of the charges against Oppenheimer. In the meantime, the president ordered that a "blank wall" be placed between the scientist and any classified information. This decision was controversial and of little value; much of the information denied Oppenheimer was the result of his own research.[13] Strauss established a review board, and Oppenheimer agreed to the investigation when he returned from a European trip. The board consisted of Gordon Gray, formerly secretary of the army under Truman and at the time president of the University of North Carolina; Thomas Morgan, the past president of Sperry Corporation;

and Ward Evans, a chemistry professor at Loyola University. The board conducted its investigation throughout the spring of 1954. Its final decision on 27 May stated that Oppenheimer was a loyal citizen but a "security risk" because of his past associations with Communists and his effort to impede research on the hydrogen bomb. The Atomic Energy Commission upheld the board's verdict and revoked Oppenheimer's security clearance.[14]

The commission's decision and its handling of the case brought immediate protests from the scientific community. Some of Oppenheimer's friends charged that Strauss engineered the decision because of personal animosity against the scientist. David Lilienthal, a pioneer in nuclear research, claimed that Strauss and Oppenheimer had violently disagreed over the future direction of research on the hydrogen bomb, and Oppenheimer had infuriated Strauss with that opposition. Eisenhower and Strauss maintained the opposite, however, with each man claiming that personal motives played no role in the decision. In his memoirs, Strauss contended that "the decision was agonizing . . . for the men who had to make it," but ruled out any personal distaste for Oppenheimer. Eisenhower spoke of Strauss as a man of "distinction, integrity and selflessness."[15]

The Oppenheimer hearings marked one of the few occasions when Wilson chose to be less than candid with the press. On two separate occasions during press conferences, he declined to respond to questions which dealt with the hearings. On 14 April, when asked whether he could discuss the Oppenheimer situation, he replied, "I shouldn't comment on it," and proceeded to explain the administration's overall approach to the internal security problem. On 18 April, he stated that the case was being "reviewed by a proper board" and refused to confirm the "blank wall" decision.[16]

The Eisenhower administration's handling of the Oppenheimer case was certainly less than ideal. That particular scientist's genius had contributed greatly to American military capability. The decision to revoke his security clearance tainted Oppenheimer in the public mind, although he later secured an appointment at the Institute for Advanced Study at Princeton University. Even though the early 1950s were emotionally charged times, when respect for individual rights was certainly not a paramount concern, Oppenheimer deserved better treatment.[17] Furthermore, the administration damaged itself by authorizing an investigation of him. By ordering an examination rather than discretely removing the scientist from government service, Eisenhower left the impression that the administration feared McCarthy and that it would go to any length to placate him. If such was the case, McCarthy confounded the attempt. He was beyond appeasement, and, in early 1954, began his attack on the Army's security system. In what Eisenhower later termed McCarthy's "last and most ambitious attack," the senator began with an investigation of a so-called espionage plot at Fort Monmouth, New Jersey, and finished with a full-scale assault on the Army's leadership in front of the television cameras and a national viewing audience.[18]

McCarthy's investigation at Fort Monmouth in late 1953 collapsed without evidence of any subversives. But the senator refused to cancel the inquiry into the Army's practices. In January 1954, McCarthy learned that Dr. Irving Peress, a dentist stationed at Camp Kilmer, New Jersey, had been promoted to officer status. This action was taken in accordance with the Doctor Draft Act. When the Army later learned that Peress was a member of the leftist American Labor party in New York, it ordered his discharge within ninety days. As Herbert S. Parmet wrote, McCarthy was delighted that he had finally found a "real" Communist and demanded, "Who promoted Peress?"[19] He called the dentist to appear before a closed session of his subcommittee of the Government Operations Committee. Peress objected to McCarthy's harassment and requested the Army to grant him his discharge. The Army happily complied.

In accordance with its regulations, the Army granted Peress an honorable discharge. McCarthy immediately cried conspiracy and maintained that the Army leadership protected Peress from further examination by dismissing him. Peress, who refused to answer a number of questions in McCarthy's 30 January session, was a "Fifth Amendment Communist," or so the senator stated. He demanded that Secretary of the Army Stevens and General Ralph Zwicker, the commander at Camp Kilmer, testify before his committee. Alarmed at McCarthy's latest outrage, Stevens visited the White House on 10 February and spoke with Eisenhower. After Stevens explained the Army's handling of the case, the president told him to admit any administrative error and cooperate with the committee. But Eisenhower instructed the secretary not to endure any of McCarthy's bullying tactics, and, if insulted, to leave the hearing.[20]

McCarthy continued his investigations into the Peress case throughout February. On 18 February, he questioned Peress, General Zwicker, and three other officers from Camp Kilmer. During that session, Peress refused to answer thirty-three questions, which infuriated McCarthy. The senator lashed out at Zwicker and the other officers for their supposed "stupidity" in not recognizing that Peress was a "subversive." Referring to the general as a man "who didn't have the brains of a five-year-old," McCarthy charged that Zwicker "was not fit to wear the uniform."[21]

Such humiliation of a military officer enraged the administration. Eisenhower, who knew Zwicker during World War II and witnessed his bravery during the Battle of the Bulge, began to consider some means of stopping McCarthy. Wilson, too, condemned the Wisconsin senator during a press conference on 4 March. "General Zwicker wasn't treated as courteously as he was entitled," the secretary stated.[22]

Reacting to McCarthy's boorishness, Stevens ordered Zwicker not to appear before the senator's investigation and announced his intention to appear in the general's place. When confronted with Stevens's statement, McCarthy went into a rage. He telephoned the secretary of the army, warning him not to prohibit Zwicker's future testimony. In a bellicose manner, McCarthy challenged Stevens "to just go ahead and try it. . . . I am going to kick the brains out of anyone who protects Communists! You just go ahead, Robert. I guarantee that you will live to regret it."[23] Furthermore, he vowed to make a public example of Zwicker on national television if the Army did not cooperate with his investigation.

Stevens was in a difficult position. After following Eisenhower's instructions, he had witnessed McCarthy's growing unreasonableness. His own Army subordinates, including Chief of Staff Ridgway, pressured him to support Zwicker against McCarthy's attacks. He therefore decided to attend a "secret" luncheon with McCarthy in an effort to patch up the situation and bring some order back to the dissension-ridden GOP. He did not inform either Eisenhower or Wilson of his intentions. Held on 24 February in Senator Everett Dirksen's office, this meeting offered Stevens and McCarthy the opportunity to make amends. The secretary received the senator's agreement to cancel the televised investigation and treat any officer under examination with respect. But, unfortunately, the meeting had ceased to be a secret. When the group adjourned, it found press photographers stationed in the hallway and reporters eager for answers as to the nature of the meeting. McCarthy grinned and threw his arm around Stevens, who smiled wanly as the cameras clicked.

Although Stevens thought he had accomplished his objective of persuading McCarthy to stop brow-beating Army witnesses, that was not to be the case. McCarthy reported that Stevens had surrendered to his every demand, as if he had "gotten down on his knees."[24] Immediately, the press flashed the word that the Eisenhower administration had relented to McCarthy's demands for more information and more testimony. Stevens feared that he might have to resign. But the administration had not relented. In fact, the opposite course was already set. Through late February and into early March, the administration plotted its response to McCarthy, now considered too dangerous for any further tolerance.

On 25 February, White House Chief of Staff Sherman Adams, with the assistance of Vice-president Nixon and presidential aide Jerry Persons, issued a statement clarifying the true nature of Stevens's discussions with McCarthy. In early March, Eisenhower spoke with a group of Republican congressmen about the futility of fighting communism by "destroying the things in which we believe."[25]

Wilson also spoke out against McCarthy. At a press conference on 4 March, the secretary dealt with the McCarthy problem. Discussing the Peress case, Wilson said, "This left-wing dentist was certainly no great security risk." Furthermore, he firmly rejected the senator's charge that the Army was "coddling Communists," noting that "the Army has been fighting Communists in Korea." When asked if he agreed with McCarthy that known Communists in the armed services should be placed in forced-labor camps, Wilson replied, "I doubt if that is the solution. I don't want to be a party to a witch-hunt." The secretary offered one other piece of information that proved to be the highlight of the conference: his department would provide any information which it had concerning McCarthy's alleged pressuring of Army personnel for favored treatment for a GI named G. David Schine, formerly a McCarthy staff member.[26]

When confronted with Wilson's decision, McCarthy angrily accused the Pentagon and the Army of trying to divert the investigation "over to the Navy and Air Force."[27] But soon the Senate made preparations for the opening round of the Army-McCarthy Hearings, a spectacle that was to occupy two months, beginning in late April and ending in mid-June.

Wilson closely monitored the course of those hearings but was only indirectly involved in them. He and McCarthy clashed only once prior to the start of the hearings, and that apparently convinced the senator that this secretary of defense had no intention of suffering indignities. On 10 March, Wilson and McCarthy met at the Pentagon, where the senator attempted to force the secretary's appearance at the hearings. But Wilson refused, unless specific instances were offered which showed that his testimony was necessary. "I didn't come down here to be a television actor," he told McCarthy. For his part, the senator relented and said that he and Wilson were not quarreling. "Mr. Wilson has been fighting Communists for longer than I," he stated.[28]

While the Army-McCarthy Hearings were in progress, the secretary of defense attended to other matters relating to internal security, among them the amendment of the Doctor Draft Act in order to prevent another Peress case. A federal court had recently ruled that physicians were entitled to commissions based on their training unless they refused to complete the loyalty questionnaire required for entry into the armed services.[29] McCarthy had attacked the Army's security procedures and Wilson wished to make changes in the internal security policy which would conform to legal rulings. As it stood, the act required that physicians be granted commissions because of their professional training. Like other military personnel, they were given loyalty questionnaires which determined their suitability for military service. Unless charged specifically with an act of wrongdoing while in the armed services, they were eligible for honorable discharge. The Army's error in the Peress case, if indeed it was an error, involved his induction and promotion even though he was a member of the left-wing American Labor party. The Army acted correctly in discharging him. Wilson never considered Peress a security risk simply because of his past political membership in the American Labor party. McCarthy, however, made it appear that the Army had failed to detect a known Communist within its ranks, and had discharged him only after the senator began to investigate the matter. McCarthy claimed that the Army not only had lax security procedures, but that it had attempted to hide its errors rather than admit them.

Wilson's proposal to amend the Doctor Draft Act contained two significant provisions. First, it stipulated that any physician who failed the loyalty review would be placed in enlisted status, ineligible for promotion, until he qualified by passing the security standard. Second, the amendment spelled out in detail the specific criteria to be used in determining whether an individual was a security risk.[30] Wilson appeared before the Senate Armed Services Committee on two occasions, 18 March and 8 April, to offer his defense of the proposal. Each time, he reported that the Defense Department's security problem was small and that its review procedures were sound. He maintained that his amendment was designed to improve and clarify those procedures.

But the questioning which Wilson received from the members of the committee showed how tightly McCarthyism had gripped the Senate. Lyndon Johnson asked Wilson to provide his estimate of the number of loyalty suspects in the armed services. Furthermore, Johnson speculated that the error which occurred in the Army's handling of the Peress case may have been due to a relaxation of loyalty procedures. Nor was Johnson the only Democrat who questioned Wilson's administration of loyalty procedures. Estes Kefauver, whose investigations into organized crime had occupied national attention in 1951, informed Wilson that Congress stood ready to examine the Pentagon if the secretary's policies failed. Another Wilson antagonist, Stuart Symington, expressed concern that the Pentagon's security procedures would not allay public apprehension about the extent of subversive influence. Republican senators were, of course, exceedingly reluctant to stray from McCarthy's position. John Sherman Cooper wondered about the impact of any Communist influence on morale in the armed services. Margaret Chase Smith, who was known to disapprove of McCarthy's tactics, nevertheless wanted Wilson's assurance that no evidence of "Communist coddling" existed.[31]

The 18 March hearings were significant for several reasons. First, they demonstrated that few senators were willing publicly to oppose McCarthy. Second, the questioning demonstrated that most of the members of the committee accepted McCarthy's charge that the Army's security procedures were poor and that the proposal which Wilson offered was insufficient to protect the national interest. With his initial testimony a failure, Wilson returned to the Pentagon and instructed his aides to improve the proposal. On 7 April, the secretary issued a directive to all the service branches and departments which clarified his policy about the physicians and internal security. In that directive, Wilson put the Department of Defense squarely on the side of due process for servicemen accused of being security risks.[32]

On 8 April, the secretary testified before the Senate Armed Services Committee for the second time about the amendment to the Doctor Draft Act, which this time contained the provisions of the 7 April directive. He disclosed that known Communists or subversives would not be drafted, but those who violated the loyalty standards would be dealt with fairly. Discussing the complications involved in administering a security review, Wilson observed:

> The loyalty business gets difficult between charging a man with disloyalty and proving that he is disloyal, as against saying he is a security risk. That is one reason why we don't want to be too tough on the conditions under which we let them out. But here is a man, on account of his affiliation and way of thinking is a risk. We can't use him in the service because we have to have more people watching him than he does us any good. We don't want to smear him for life, but we want to get him out of the service.
> These procedures will get the job done.[33]

The questioning which Wilson received from the senators was very different in the 8 April from that on 18 March. In the March session, the committee members questioned whether the Pentagon's security system provided the necessary means to find subversives, but in April they wondered whether the regulations granted an accused subversive his constitutional rights. Their basic concern was whether an accused serviceman would have the opportunity to appeal a verdict. Wilson assured the senators that any serviceman charged with being a security risk could appeal a verdict against him. He pointed out that an accused GI could appeal to two military boards, the Board of Review of Discharges and the Board of Correction of Military Records. But that assurance failed to satisfy the committee. Some committee members, such as Senator Kefauver, maintained that a civilian as well as a military appeal board was necessary. Wilson tentatively agreed that a civilian board might be acceptable but resented the implication that the services' judicial policies were insufficient. He feared that another civilian investigation would accelerate the decline in morale already evident in the Army. Furthermore, the State Department had not experienced positive results when Dulles allowed McLeod to examine its security files. In short, Wilson argued that the time was not appropriate for more outside investigations into the procedures of the military establishment.[34]

Congress debated the proposed amendments to the Doctor Draft Act through late April and May. In mid-June, the law was extended through 1955, with Wilson's amendments included in the final passage.[35] This legislative achievement was significant; Wilson had changed the Defense Department's security procedure with congressional advice and consent. Unlike Dulles, he did not resort to arbitrary decrees because of pressure from the GOP's right wing.

The Army-McCarthy Hearings, of course, ran concurrently with Wilson's efforts to amend the Doctor Draft Act. While the secretary of defense tried to persuade Congress to enact the amendments, Secretary of the Army Robert Stevens endured McCarthy's questioning for thirty-five days. Essentially the hearings dealt with one issue: did McCarthy and Roy Cohn, the senator's administrative assistant, use undue influence to pressure the Army leadership into giving special treatment to Schine, or were the Army's charges fabricated to destroy the senator's career? As the hearings progressed, it became evident that McCarthy was in a vulnerable position. Stevens, who was defended by a skillful Boston lawyer named Joseph Welch, presented evidence which showed the chronology of McCarthy's intervention on Schine's behalf. The senator, increasingly on the defensive, could only lash out at Defense Department personnel and interrupt the proceedings with "points of order." Welch, whose courtroom manner was impeccable, repeatedly subjected McCarthy to rhetorical humiliation.[36]

Wilson had only peripheral contact with the hearings. He emphasized his confidence in the Army leadership during a number of press conferences, and on 17 March, prior to the opening of the hearings, he issued a statement supporting Stevens. Maintaining that he "had no reservations about Stevens' integrity," Wilson repeated his intention to provide the Senate with the information the Pentagon had collected against the senator's activities.[37] On 11 May, Wilson supported Stevens again, maintaining that the Army's security system was excellent and McCarthy's probe only served to lower morale in the services.[38]

Wilson found it necessary on other occasions to defend Pentagon personnel who were under attack by McCarthy. One such case involved Assistant Secretary of Defense Struve Hensel, charged by McCarthy with profiteering. He maintained that Hensel had used his position as a procurement official during World War II to place government contracts with firms in which he held an interest, and alleged that Hensel blocked his investigation of the matter after the war. This accounted for the attacks on him by the Army and the Defense Department, McCarthy maintained. Hensel responded by saying that the senator's allegations were "bare-faced lies."[39] He challenged McCarthy to repeat the charges outside the confines of the Senate, whereupon, Hensel vowed, he would sue for libel. McCarthy, of course, refused to do so.

McCarthy had originally made those charges in a bill of particulars against the Army which he filed with Government Operations Subcommittee Chairman Karl Mundt before the opening of the hearings. On 21 April, Wilson discussed Hensel's business practices during a press conference. In his words: "Struve Hensel is a competent, honest man and if I didn't believe so, he wouldn't be in his present assignment. . . . I am satisfied with the explanation of his business interests."[40] The secretary of defense left determinations of "positive loyalty" to Dulles and McLeod.

The closest that Wilson came to direct involvement in the hearings occurred in early May. At that time, McCarthy produced a letter which he said had been written by FBI Director Hoover, claiming that the Army should be aware of security violations at Fort Monmouth. The senator stated that he received the letter from an Army intelligence officer who went beyond his orders in turning the letter over to him. Hoover denied having signed the letter, and McCarthy refused to give the name of the officer. Senator Mundt then contacted Eisenhower and asked the president for guidance. In a controversial decision, Eisenhower decided to claim executive privilege and withhold any information about the matter from the committee. In a letter written to Wilson on 17 May, Eisenhower stated his belief in protecting confidentiality between members of the executive branch.

Because it is necessary to efficient and effective administration that employees of the executive branch be in a position to be completely candid in advising with each other on official matters, and because it is not in the public interest that any of their conversations or communications, or any documents or reproductions, concerning such advice be disclosed, you will instruct employees of your Department that in all of their appearances before the Subcommittee of the Senate Committee on Government Operations regarding the inquiry now before it that they are not to testify to any such conversations or communications or to produce any documents or reproductions. This principle must be maintained regardless of who would be benefited by such disclosures.

As Eisenhower recalled in his memoirs, this instruction to Wilson brought a cry of outrage from McCarthy. The senator labeled the president's action a "black-out" and "cover-up." But the president stated: "As distasteful as such action was, I deemed it essential and I made it stick."[41]

The Army-McCarthy Hearings ended on 17 June. It became obvious that McCarthy's reputation and standing within the Republican party had been severely damaged. Stevens emerged with his reputation enhanced. Joseph Welch distinguished himself, not only for his superb defense of Stevens, but also for his skillful handling of McCarthy's parliamentary boorishness. In the following autumn, the Senate censured McCarthy for his actions, a further blow to his public credibility.

Thus the senator found that the Army-McCarthy Hearings marked the beginning of his decline. Throughout the summer, however, he continued his anti-Communist remonstrances. In early August, McCarthy even threatened to reopen the Peress case. But Wilson had tired of such matters. When asked in a press conference if he had any new comment on the Peress case, Wilson replied, "I have no comment on the Peress case. I thought that was all past. I have more important things to do than keep hashing that one over." The secretary was particularly impatient with those who wanted "to hash over old problems." He considered such exercises futile, "like making birth control retro-active."[42]

Wilson's behavior during the McCarthy period was significant. He never embraced the anti-Communist issue nor used it as a means of personal aggrandizement. In fact, he considered the time spent searching for subversives and conducting loyalty investigations as virtually unnecessary. More important, Wilson never brandished McCarthyism over the heads of Pentagon colleagues to compel compliance with his policies. Unlike the State Department, the Defense Department never experienced a witch-hunt. When the Pentagon's leadership was under attack, Wilson supported the department. He defended Hensel and Stevens from some of McCarthy's most unconscionable smears. In addition, the secretary spoke highly of the Defense Department in his public speeches during this time, as in his address before the 1954 national convention of the Chamber of Commerce in Washington.

> There is still lots to be done, and we face new and important problems every day. But I just want to go on record with all of you, and I have known many of you for years, that the Defense Team is not discouraged. We seem to have survived the "snow treatment." In spite of the magnitude of the job, we have made progress in solving many of our difficult problems, while facing, may I add, *some less important and time-consuming ones.* We have made real progress in providing our nation with a sound defense program. We have no frustrations and our morale is good [emphasis added].[43]

Several writers have noted Eisenhower's reluctance to become personally involved in stopping McCarthy's investigations.[44] Seen in retrospect, this was a shortcoming on the president's part. Yet it is true that once Eisenhower moved against McCarthy, the senator was doomed. That effort began when the Army, with Wilson's permission, released its bill of particulars against the senator. These documents proved conclusively that McCarthy and his staff did pressure the Army leadership to grant special treatment to Schine. Furthermore, Eisenhower's assertion of executive privilege, and Wilson's refusal to permit any Pentagon employee to testify before the Operations Committee subcommittee unless officially charged, prevented McCarthy from continuing his slurs against honest public servants.

One should not misunderstand, however; Charles E. Wilson did not ruin Joseph McCarthy. Indeed, given Wilson's temperament, he probably did not even wish to. Yet the secretary did play a significant, if somewhat unnoticed part, in the senator's self-destruction. The reasons behind Wilson's opposition to McCarthy are somewhat unclear. Perhaps the secretary's commonsense approach to administration precluded any panicky hunting for subversives. A more probable reason, however, was Wilson's political position within the administration. He owed little to the Republican right wing. Admittedly a conservative, Wilson based his conservatism on fiscal restraint and limited government, not domestic anti-Communism. He was in some ways fortunate in that regard; McCarthy's supporters failed to devote as much attention to looking for Communists in the Pentagon as they did in the State Department. At any rate, Wilson conceived of his responsibilities as making progress in the defense operation, not hunting subversives.

For the secretary, the events of 1954 would have been tumultuous even without McCarthy's attacks. It was in 1954 that the administration presented its first military budget, and Wilson was the guardian and defender of the so-called New Look in the political arena. For the next three years, his advocacy of this military program proved to be one of the most controversial aspects of the political history of the Eisenhower administration.

6

Wilson and the New Look

W ITH the end of the Korean War in 1953, the Eisenhower administration turned its attention to the formulation of its own national defense program. A number of critical decisions needed to be made if President Eisenhower and Secretary of Defense Wilson were to develop a defense policy consistent with the administration's overall economic and national security objectives. Wilson had given the nation an indication of the future course of defense policy during 1953, when he succeeded in eliminating some nonessential military spending. Although these reductions squared with the president's desire to streamline the military establishment and make it more effective, the cutbacks occurred in a Pentagon budget submitted by former President Harry Truman. It was not until 1954 that Eisenhower presented a military program which bore his own imprint.

The president unveiled that program, referred to as the New Look, in his State of the Union address in January 1954. The origins of this particular military policy were complex. Prior to his inauguration, Eisenhower spoke with several of his cabinet appointees about a future military program. The most intensive discussions on the matter occurred on Eisenhower's return trip from Korea in December 1952, aboard the U.S.S. *Helena,* and involved Eisenhower, Wilson, John Foster Dulles, George M. Humphrey, Joseph Dodge, the prospective director of the Bureau of the Budget, and Admiral Arthur Radford. Although these discussions gave Eisenhower the opportunity to explore a future military program, he made no firm decision about its components.

The actual planning began in midsummer 1953. After the selection of the new Joint Chiefs of Staff, Eisenhower instructed them to reappraise the entire defense program. (Hence the term "New Look," as the Joint Chiefs were reexamining an existing policy.) They prepared their study throughout the summer (the bulk of their discussions taking place during a four-day cruise in August on the *Sequoia*, the yacht belonging to the secretary of the navy), without benefit of staff, and tried to reach agreement on a military plan which guaranteed security at an affordable cost.[1] The military leaders completed the report in late summer and presented it to Wilson on 2 October. In their recommendations, they included a planned reduction in manpower for the Army and Navy, increases in funding and force levels for the Air Force, an improved continental defense program, and a renewed commitment to research and development funds for nuclear research and technology. The estimated cost for this program was $34.5 billion in the coming fiscal year.[2]

Wilson and Radford presented these recommendations to the president in a meeting of the National Security Council on 13 October. They were, in a sense, the bearers of bad tidings. Humphrey and Dodge had envisioned a defense expenditure of $30 billion or less. The amount which Radford and Wilson recommended was roughly the same as the current level of military spending, and Humphrey wondered whether the imperatives of the administration's domestic program—a balanced budget, tax cut, and reduced federal spending—would be possible if the Pentagon continued to spend such great amounts. So Wilson was requested to do some additional economizing. The secretary of defense and Admiral Radford did make some additional reductions, and in a significant way. At the next National Security Council meeting on 30 October, Radford explained that more economies were possible if the military was allowed to use nuclear weapons where it "was technologically feasible."[3] Given that permission, Radford argued that the Joint Chiefs of Staff would not need to plan for such diverse strategic eventualities as limited warfare and guerrilla insurgencies. Nuclear weapons could serve as options in such examples of limited warfare as the Korean conflict.

Radford's thinking regarding the role of nuclear weapons in the administration's defense policy took shape as the subject of the National Security Council's position paper, NSC 162/2. The decision to rely on nuclear weaponry and technology instead of a large, powerfully equipped, standing army became the backbone of the New Look. NSC 162/2 contended that the products of recent atomic research could be used in military programming as a deterrent to war, as protection against attack, and as the primary American offensive weapons. By the end of 1953, it was evident that the administration intended to propose that Congress agree to reductions in overall defense spending and cutbacks in manpower but to increased funding for nuclear research and air power.

It was also clear that five members of the administration were predominantly responsible for the direction of military policy. Foremost of the five was Eisenhower, who had decided that economic considerations were integral to military programming. In some respects, the president's demand for a cost-conscious military program was conditioned by political factors. As a presidential candidate, he had promised to reduce spending and cut federal taxes. Significant progress in both of these areas was impossible without some belt-tightening at the Pentagon. But beyond that, Eisenhower was genuinely concerned about the potential negative effects which large military outlays could exert on a free economy. In *The Living Presidency,* Emmett John Hughes, one of Eisenhower's assistants and his major speech writer, recalled the president's thoughts on this subject shortly after he took office.

"The jet plane that roars over your head costs three-quarters of a million dollars. That is more money than a man earning ten thousand dollars every year is going to make in his lifetime. What world can afford this sort of thing for long? We are in an armaments race. Where will it lead us? At worst, to atomic warfare. At best, to robbing every nation and people on earth of the fruits of their own toil.

Now there could be another road before us—the road of disarmament. What does this mean? It means for everybody in the world bread, butter, clothes, homes, hospitals, schools, all the good and necessary things for decent living. So let this be the choice we offer. Let us talk straight; no double talk, no sophisticated political formulas, no slick propaganda devices. Let us spell it out, whatever we truly offer."[4]

As the secretary of defense, Wilson was obviously a significant figure in the implementation of the administration's defense program,

Secretary of State John Foster Dulles making a point during the televised cabinet meeting held in November 1954. Wilson appears to be somewhat skeptical.

By permission of the Wilson Archives

and he shared Eisenhower's concern about skyrocketing military costs. "The idea that Defense business is prosperity just isn't so," he once stated. "It's no good when a community leans on Defense work. It was a policy of production for consumption that made this nation great."[5] In his official capacity as the New Look's public defender, Wilson argued that any reductions in military spending were sound if they did not damage the nation's defense posture. Furthermore, these reductions would have a positive impact on the civilian economy and thereby contribute to the nation's overall strength.

The chief military adviser to President Eisenhower and Secretary Wilson, Admiral Radford also possessed significant influence during the 1950s. The chairman of the Joint Chiefs between 1953 and 1957, Radford was the military officer in charge of implementing the New Look's strategic objectives. During his tenure, the Air Force received responsibilities both as a continental defender and as the nation's primary means of retaliation. These increased responsibilities were to bring the Air Force a sizable increase in its share of military appropriations, while the roles, missions, and funding of the Army and Navy declined appreciably.

In addition to Eisenhower, Wilson, and Radford, Secretary of the Treasury Humphrey and Secretary of State Dulles played key roles in determining defense policy. Humphrey's role was especially significant. Stephen Ambrose and Walter LaFeber have shown how Humphrey's suspicion of heavy government spending so influenced Eisenhower's thinking that his advice extended beyond economic policy into the area of defense policy. In retrospect, it is evident that Wilson and Humphrey acted to restrain large increases in defense spending. In Ambrose's words, "The Republicans were more determined to balance the budget than they were to support a war machine."[6]

Given the fact that the New Look, in the thinking of Eisenhower, Humphrey, and Wilson, was a defensive strategy, designed to protect the nation and to act as a deterrent to large-scale aggression, Dulles often had a negative effect on the public's understanding of the administration's defense program. The most visible and vocal member of the Eisenhower cabinet, Dulles had a tendency to issue stern warnings to the Communist nations about the serious consequences of threatening the United States. In a major foreign policy address to the Council on Foreign Relations on 17 January 1954, Dulles spoke of America's potential for "massive retaliation" in the event of Communist aggression. The address had a particularly negative effect, picturing the United States as a superpower threatening destruction to those who opposed its policies. It served to portray the New Look as an offensive strategy, obscuring its defensive and economic rationale, and implied that the United States was prepared to risk a nuclear confrontation with the Soviets.[7] Unfortunately, Dulles gave his "massive retaliation" speech at about the same time that Eisenhower introduced the New Look in his address to Congress, thereby creating some public confusion about the administration's defense objectives. The subsequent strident rhetoric of the secretary of state, who also was to speak of "liberation," "rollback," "agonizing reappraisal," and "brinkmanship," did not keep the administration from attempting to carry out the basic goals of the policy, however. Humphrey's concern for economy exerted a powerful restraint on the oratory of the secretary of state when policy matters were discussed. As Walter LaFeber has written, "At each Cabinet meeting in which Dulles defended the free world against Communism, Humphrey defended the treasury against the prodigals, especially those who wanted larger budgets for conventional forces. Dulles acquiesced in these views."[8]

In summary, the military program which the administration presented to Congress in 1954 and 1955 emphasized an increased commitment to nuclear research and technology, a reduction in manpower, and control of military costs. Even so, the costs of national defense were high, and, as Eisenhower and Wilson admitted, would remain high for the next several years. The administration recognized that the Communist threat would continue indefinitely and believed that the New Look, with its various emphases, would serve the nation best over the "long haul."[9]

Congress might have been more receptive to the New Look were it not for the administration's firm emphasis on economy. Admittedly many congressmen were conservative during the early 1950s, and they shared Eisenhower's views on limiting federal expenditures. But as the tensions of the Cold War continued, aggravated by what many in Congress and the press perceived to be Russian threats to the security of Western Europe and uncertainty over Communist China's intentions in Asia, speculation arose that the administration was spending too little on national defense. As fear of increasing Russian military strength grew during the years 1954 to 1956, the pressures mounted for Wilson to submit a higher defense budget. Nevertheless, Eisenhower and Wilson sought to hold down defense costs, and, in 1954 and 1955, held firm against both Democratic and Republican critics who felt that the administration's plans were insufficient to protect the nation.

The administration presented the details of the first New Look budget to Congress in late January 1954. Wilson appeared before the Subcommittee on Defense Appropriations of the House Appropriations Committee on 1 February. In his testimony, he emphasized that reductions in military spending were possible if the Pentagon practiced economy in three different areas: planning, programming, and operation. In referring to economy in planning, Wilson discussed the administration's approach to the size of the armed forces. The emphasis on new weapons systems meant that the number of personnel in the various services could be reduced. The secretary also pointed out that one element of the New Look was a proposal for the enactment of a qualitative reserve plan. Congressional approval of such a plan would lower operating costs by allowing further reduction of the number of full-time military personnel. Economy in programming required a functional balance between all the elements of the military operation. Unification of the armed services would be the ideal means of achieving that goal, but the separate branches had resisted any proposals for unification since the Truman years. Thus, Wilson's goal was to insure proper coordination between the services and eliminate, insofar as possible, their quarreling and competition for ever larger appropriations. By economy in operation, Wilson meant that he intended to curtail waste, duplication, and inefficiency in the military program. This task, the secretary said, was "a continuous one which involved getting the right man in the right place at the right time."[10]

Wilson continued his defense of the New Look before Congress throughout March. On 15 March, he testified before the Senate Subcommittee on Defense Appropriations.

The members of the Appropriations Committee were concerned

mainly with Wilson's answers to questions about the budgetary impact of the New Look. The secretary justified the reductions in manpower and funding by stating that some defense costs and manpower levels could be reduced due to the end of the Korean War. He maintained, however, that the cost of national security would remain high for the foreseeable future. Wilson again emphasized that the administration believed that the level of defense spending needed to be one that the nation could afford: "Over the long pull, economic strength is an indispensable pre-requisite for military strength." At another point in this testimony, he discussed the difference between programs which would be emphasized and those which would be reevaluated. Programs involving electronics, guided missile operations, and work in research and development stood to receive additional funding. The Pentagon hoped to economize on its conventional warfare components, however.[11]

After explaining the spending levels of this military budget, Wilson discussed its strategic impact. In his statement to the senators, he sought to allay any concern over the administration's policy on nuclear weapons, pointing out that the nation's atomic arsenal was developed primarily as a deterrent to war and not designed for any particular offensive purpose. Regarding the proposed reductions in Army troop strength, the secretary maintained that historically the United States had sought to substitute mechanical developments for human labor and that the military establishment was following that precedent. Furthermore, new technological innovations were bringing about a new relationship between men and machines for military purposes.[12]

The senators pursued the various facets of the New Look in their questioning. Homer Ferguson, the subcommittee chairman and a supporter of the administration, asked Wilson to clarify further the Pentagon's position regarding the use of nuclear weapons. Wilson answered that the Pentagon did not rely solely on its atomic capability and that conventional warfare strategy still figured in the military equation, although it was less important. In the event of nuclear war, the president intended to notify both Congress and the nation's allies before undertaking any retaliation. Finally, Wilson assured Ferguson that the administration's first priority in submitting the defense

budget was national security, not economy. Democrats on the subcommittee then questioned some of the administration's assumptions
about national security. Burnett Maybank of South Carolina disagreed with Wilson's decision to reduce Army troop strength, arguing
that any reserve plan, however soon it might be enacted, was no
substitute for a large standing army. In his view, the nation stood to
gain more by keeping a larger army until future Communist intentions were better understood.[13]

Wilson finished his congressional testimony in April and May, and
Congress began formal consideration of the New Look during early
June. The GOP controlled both houses of Congress, a fact which
certainly worked to the administration's advantage. Furthermore,
several Republican legislators, along with some southern Democrats,
were more conservative on economic policy than Eisenhower and
Wilson, even when it involved national defense. Thus the administration possessed the necessary political strength in 1954 not only to
insure the passage of its military program but also to defeat any significant changes which the opposition might want to make in it.

Several liberal Democrats spoke out against the New Look, however. On 16 June, a day of intense debate about the military program,
several Democrats voiced their criticism. Led by Stuart Symington,
John F. Kennedy, Hubert Humphrey, and Lyndon Johnson, the opposition called for an increased appropriation for the Army and re-
storation of the cutbacks in manpower. Symington said the New Look
budget was insufficient to meet the nation's needs. "Survival is more
important than money," he stated. He then proposed, with Kennedy
acting as a cosponsor for the bill, that the Senate appropriate an
additional $350 million for the Army so that service could raise its
troop strength. Hubert Humphrey, in an impassioned speech, declared:

> It does no good to talk about mass retaliation. It does not do any good to
> talk about something going to happen which is not going to happen. We have
> had our bluff called two or three times in the last month [over American
> involvement in Indochina to prevent a French defeat]. We have been de-
> feated at Geneva. The first mistake was made last year, in April, 1953, when
> our officials went to the NATO Conference and stated to the European
> powers that the [military force] objectives would be stretched out for a few

By permission of *The Washington Star*

more years and for them to take it easy. I think it is now evident when we ask them to sit down at a bargaining table with the Soviets or any satellites we have to be in a position of strength. Our representatives went to Geneva after the budget had been cut and there had been put into effect a reduction in the Air Forces, when we were in Geneva with our allies, and we came home defeated.[14]

Administration supporters, however, combined to defeat the Democratic amendment to the defense budget. Sponsored by Senators Symington, Humphrey, Kennedy, Albert Gore of Tennessee, Mike Mansfield of Montana, and Mike Monroney of Oklahoma, it suggested adding two more divisions to the seventeen the administration proposed for the Army. By a thirty-eight to fifty vote, the Senate turned down the measure, with influential southern Democrats such as Harry Flood Byrd and John Stennis joining the Republican majority.[15] Shortly thereafter, the Senate passed H.R. 8873, which authorized defense expenditures for the coming fiscal year. After Senate passage on 17 June, the House gave its approval on 25 June to a proposed Pentagon budget of $29.2 billion.[16] This final figure was actually $2 billion less than the administration originally requested. The New Look had survived its first political test with the administration's goals for it virtually intact.

Although the administration managed to guide the first New Look budget through Congress in 1954, it could not deny that its Democratic opposition had raised some issues about the defense program which might cause some public alarm. In retrospect, one can argue that Wilson and Eisenhower made the correct decision in reducing defense expenditures. During the mid-1950s, America's strategic superiority over the Soviet Union was impressive, even though security forbade a public statement of the nation's total military strength. Yet in the post-Korea and McCarthy period, national fears of the Soviet military threat were great. To many congressmen, or at least to those who were unwilling to accept the administration's analysis of the world situation or the capability of American arms, it seemed extremely dangerous to reduce defense spending at a time when Communist intentions posed a threat to the free world.

In the 1954 congressional elections, the Democrats regained control of Congress. The Republican electoral defeat compounded Wilson's political problems as secretary of defense. With the Democrats reorganizing the Congress, Wilson would be forced to deal with committee chairmen who belonged to the opposition. That problem was especially acute in the Senate with the Armed Services Committee. Leverett Saltonstall lost his chairmanship to Richard Russell, the Democrat from Georgia, and Russell was one of Wilson's critics. Furthermore, Homer Ferguson lost his Senate race in Michigan to the Democratic candidate, Patrick McNamara, and thus the administration lost another vocal supporter of its military program.[17] So the administration anticipated a difficult struggle over the 1956 Pentagon budget when it was presented to Congress in early 1955. Eisenhower's

"George, Let Me Show You Something"

Copyright 1955 by Herblock in the *Washington Post*

respect and influence with Congress remained considerable, however, and neither he nor Wilson wanted to give the political initiative to the Democrats on such a crucial issue as national defense.

In preparation for the upcoming political battle, Wilson wrote to Eisenhower on 3 January 1955, asking for his recommendations.

> For nearly two years we have discussed the various problems relating to the Armed Services and in particular the need for the conservation and proper utilization of our manpower, both military and civilian. Just before Christmas, you again discussed the question of personnel strengths with me and the Joint Chiefs of Staff.
>
> I have found so much value in the views underlying your decisions as to the personnel strengths of the Armed Services that I wonder if you would give me the gist of them in written form. I should like very much to have them available during the next year to guide me in my consideration of those matters and to be able to make them available to all of the interested people who are considering this problem.[18]

This letter provides some clues to the administration's strategy for the expected debate over the second New Look budget. Wilson, in referring to "the need for the conservation and proper utilization of our manpower," implied that his decision to reduce troop strength was irrevocable. Furthermore, he intended to appear before the congressional committees armed with the full weight of Eisenhower's military reputation.

The president replied on 5 January, repeating his desire for economy in the Pentagon. By placing more reliance on technology than on manpower, the military establishment would be more efficient and less costly. Eisenhower stated that "because of recent scientific progress, which exerts a constantly increasing influence upon the character and conduct of war, and because America's most precious possession is the lives of her citizens, we should base our security upon military formations which make maximum use of science and technology in order to minimize numbers of men."[19]

The importance of Eisenhower's letter to Wilson was evident throughout 1955. Wilson included the major points of that directive in the statements he prepared for congressional hearings. Furthermore, he used those arguments to justify the New Look whenever he gave a public address about military policy.[20]

Although he was an ever-popular target for cartoonists, Wilson held no grudges. He collected cartoons, and invited a group of cartoonists to lunch at the Pentagon on 21 March 1955. The cartoon he is admiring was drawn by Jim Berryman and signed by several other cartoonists.

By permission of the Wilson Archives

By permission of the Wilson Archives

In late January, Wilson began the presentation of the 1956 defense budget before Congress. Anticipating some opposition to any suggestion of further manpower reductions, the secretary urged the enactment of two administration proposals which sought to strengthen the armed forces but without the large costs of a permanent standing army. These two proposals, the reserve plan which Congress had failed to enact in 1954, and a career incentive plan to help attract and retain qualified officers, constituted the administration's alternative to a larger permanent uniformed establishment. Wilson began the initial explanation of the budget in a meeting with the House Appropriations Committee on 26 January. He outlined the economies which the Defense Department hoped to achieve in the coming year and pressed for a prompt consideration of the administration's two proposals. Asking for $32.2 billion in new obligational funds, Wilson pointed out that the Army's share of the appropriation would be $7.8 billion, the Navy's $9.2 billion, and the Air Force's $14.8 billion. The remaining costs were to be distributed throughout the other operations of the Defense Department.[21]

Senate Democrats did not wait long to attack the second New Look budget. On 9 February, Russell, Symington, and Henry Jackson leveled charges at the administration's proposals, especially in the area of manpower reductions. Russell said, "This is no time to engage in any wishful thinking about Communist intentions," a sentiment which Jackson seconded. Most critical of all was Symington: "Nothing Wilson has said so far has changed my opinion that these heavy cuts in our Armed Forces are not justified from the standpoint of national security."[22] On 4 April, Deputy Secretary of Defense Robert Anderson testified in place of Wilson (who was ill) before the Senate Appropriations Committee concerning these manpower reductions, explaining that the Army and Navy would incur slight decreases in both funding and force levels and that the Air Force stood to receive increases in both areas. But he also announced that the Pentagon had reduced its military spending significantly during 1954, saving between $1 and 3 billion, which would enable it to cover any unforeseen emergencies.[23]

Congress took no significant action on the Pentagon budget during April. But on 17 May, Symington introduced an element of drama into the course of the debate. The senator made two charges, one expected and the other unexpected. First, he charged that the administration's request for ground forces was insufficient and proposed that the Senate add an additional $46 million to the Marine Corps budget. Second and more dramatic, he charged in a Senate speech "that it is now clear that in quality as well as quantity, the Soviets are surpassing the United States" in total air capability.[24] He called for an investigation of the administration's procurement program involving the B-52 heavy bomber.

Although he overestimated Soviet air might,[25] Symington's charges raised some serious questions in Washington. For two years, the Eisenhower administration had devoted top priority to the development of a powerful air component. If this program was a failure, as Symington alleged, was the administration's entire defense program a colossal mistake? Even more important, was the Soviet Union's acknowledged buildup in air strength of sufficient magnitude to generate an American response to it?

On 6 June, Wilson appeared before the Subcommittee on Defense Appropriations of the Senate Appropriations Committee to answer questions regarding the manpower reductions and alleged mismanagement of the B-52 procurement program. Appearing with the secretary were Admiral Radford and Air Force Chief of Staff General Nathan Twining. Wilson testified as to the soundness of the Pentagon's B-52 procurement operation and argued that the manpower reductions would cause no alarm if Congress passed the reserve plan. In an exchange with Allen Ellender of Louisiana, he emphasized that the large and medium-range bombers in America's arsenal presented a significant deterrent to any future invasion. After Ellender finished his questions, several other members of the committee quizzed Wilson about the status of the B-52 program. John Stennis, William Knowland, and Dennis Chavez of New Mexico informed the secretary of their misgivings about it and pointed out that an investigation might be in order. Speaking for the Defense Department, Wilson stated that he appreciated the Senate's concern about the issue but that other factors besides air power were involved in national security. Nevertheless, the subcommittee agreed to recommend an investigation of the B-52 procurement operation, a study which did not begin until the

The Eisenhower cabinet, 29 July 1955.

By permission of the Wilson Archives

following year. During the same hearings, Chavez also criticized Wilson's continued defense of reductions in Army manpower. In the recent past, Army Chief of Staff Ridgway had voiced his skepticism about decreasing the Army's role in military affairs. Chavez charged that the administration's reserve plan could not serve as a substitute for a trained standing army. Wilson replied: "So many people worship things as they are, and they don't want to change anything."[26]

Wilson's testimony notwithstanding, the administration seemed to be suffering some setbacks in its defense plans for 1955. The Democrats had raised some sensitive issues about the status of American military power, issues which had to be addressed.

When the defense budget reached formal consideration in Congress during late June, it encountered more opposition than it had the year before. Led by Symington, opposition Democrats succeeded in adding $46 million to the Marine Corps appropriation, an increase which permitted that service to raise its total troop strength from 193,000 to 215,000. But although the Democrats won that particular battle, they lost the larger war. In conference, administration supporters managed to ward off any larger increases in the overall budget. The final bill, H.R. 6042, contained an appropriation of $31.9 billion, about $200 million less than the administration had requested. Congress approved the bill on 30 June, and Eisenhower signed it into law on 13 July.[27] The opposition was forced to postpone a full-scale assault on the New Look until the following year.

The presentation, debate, and enactment of the first two New Look programs demonstrated a number of political difficulties which the Eisenhower administration faced as it entered 1956. First, some senators, usually but not invariably liberal Democrats, were growing increasingly skeptical about the administration's philosophy on national defense. Furthermore, the points that Symington, Humphrey, and others raised about the dangers of reducing Army manpower and placing too much emphasis on the Air Force had begun to find some sympathy among more conservative members of the Senate. Stennis and William Knowland, two prominent conservatives, expressed their misgivings to Wilson about the operation of the B-52 procurement procedures. Eisenhower's military reputation and congressional respect for his judgment represented the cement which held the New Look and its legislative supporters together. Secretary of Defense Wilson lacked sufficient political strength to guide the New Look through Congress without Eisenhower's backing. The general in the White House provided the New Look with a respectability it might not have had otherwise. Yet as the Democratic criticism showed, the New Look's political immunity wore thinner and thinner with each passing year.

A second political development which concerned both Eisenhower and Wilson involved the increasing hostility to the New Look from certain segments of the military. Specifically, Army leadership had begun to look with extreme disfavor on the twin evils of manpower reductions and budgetary decreases which the administration proposed. The most significant result of the Army's hostility to the New Look was that the service was moving away from the administration and seeking to state its independent case before Congress. Eisenhower and Wilson expressed private concern that the administration's critics in Congress and those in the military might cooperate to bring about public pressure for a change in defense policy.[28]

Army Chief of Staff Matthew Ridgway, for example, regarded the New Look as a poor policy. David Halberstam has noted that Ridgway counseled Eisenhower and Wilson against support of the French in Indochina during 1954. The general was concerned, not only about the tremendous logistical problems involved in an American intervention in Asia, but also because he feared that the Army lacked the capability to wage a successful operation there. Throughout his term on the Joint Chiefs, Ridgway sought help from Congress in restoring some of the Army's funding, although he did so discreetly in order to avoid a direct break with his civilian superiors. Ridgway's efforts were unsuccessful, however, and he ended his term on the JCS extremely disappointed. Resigning his appointment in June 1955, Ridgway lamented that the Army's position was "far from satisfactory."[29] Wilson selected General Maxwell D. Taylor to replace Ridgway; Taylor shared his predecessor's views on the importance of the Army's role in national defense policy.

A third and highly significant problem connected with the New Look was its reception by the public. Some elements in the media were opposed to the administration's defense policy, and Wilson was the subject of many cartoonists' barbs for his cost-cutting efforts. Would such attacks hurt the New Look in the public's eyes? The administration certainly wondered.

Although it did not appear until 1958, an article by the Yale economist James Tobin is typical of the liberal opposition to the New Look present in Washington during 1954 and 1955. The article, entitled "The Eisenhower Economy and National Security," denounced the administration on virtually every point raised in the congressional debates. Tobin was especially critical of the business managers in the cabinet and their emphasis on the economic effects of defense policy.

> We have had once more a businessman's administration, and once more it has been demonstrated that there is no one more doctrinaire and impractical in public affairs than some successful men of private affairs. The economic doctrines held by Humphrey and Wilson . . . have been the prime determinants of the Administration's budgetary and monetary policies.

The fact that Wilson and Eisenhower justified those budgetary policies as necessary to a free and uncontrolled economy and that there was little inflation seemed unimportant to Tobin.

> All good people dislike inflation, just as they oppose rainy weekends and traffic accidents. It does not follow necessarily that gradual inflation leads to runaway inflation. . . . Military strength is not achieved by making civilian goods.

Tobin also emphasized that the New Look failed to provide the nation with a military component capable to meet small-scale guerrilla insurgencies: "The United States turned its back on the concept of limited wars, and on the maintenance of the costly manpower and conventional armaments necessary to be prepared to fight them."[30]

To say that the administration "turned its back" on limited warfare was an overstatement. But both Eisenhower and Wilson contended that local defense was the primary responsibility of the nation's allies who were involved in combating Communist aggression. The president put it succinctly in *Mandate for Change:*

> The fifth important guideline was that United States security policy should take into account the need for membership in a system of alliances. Since our

resources were and are finite, we could not supply all the land, sea and air forces for the entire Free World. The logical role of our allies along the periphery of the Iron Curtain, therefore, would be to provide (with our help) for their own local security, especially ground forces, while the United States, centrally located and strong in productive power, provided mobile reserve forces of all arms, with emphasis on sea and air contingents.[31]

In considering the New Look, the administration's detractors tended to ignore the need for alliances and focused instead on the limitations of American power. Certainly it was easier to talk about the lack of conventional war capability, as Tobin did. But Eisenhower and Wilson chose to define American security in a limited way, arguing for the best use of America's finite resources.

At any rate, the administration and Congress were engaged in a test of will over the future direction of defense policy by the end of 1955. The president and the secretary of defense proposed a limited defense policy, keeping in mind the importance of a strong civilian economy. The opposition, chiefly in the Senate, claimed that national security was impossible without a more substantial military establishment. For Charles E. Wilson, sponsorship of the first two New Look budgets was a test of his political skill. That those two budgets survived Congress without drastic amendment was evidence not only of Wilson's determination to achieve their passage but also of the conservative political realities which worked in his favor. In his first three years in office, Wilson demonstrated an ability to restrain the defense budget in keeping with Eisenhower's overall national security policy. Wilson needed all the determination he could manage for the debate over the Pentagon budget in 1956. During that year, he faced full-scale political attack on the New Look as well as on his own capabilities as the secretary of defense.

7

The Opposition in Revolt: Army-Air Power Controversies

THE Eisenhower administration entered 1956 with its defense policy fairly well consolidated. Since the end of the Korean War, the military establishment had been somewhat reduced in manpower and conventional war capability but visibly strengthened in its air power and nuclear weapons components. Although the cost of national defense remained high (the request for fiscal year 1957 was $34.1 billion),[1] Defense Secretary Wilson had kept military costs fairly stable during his first three years at the Pentagon. Two New Look budgets had won congressional approval. So at first glance, the administration's New Look military program appeared to be in reasonably good condition. Wilson hoped that the Pentagon's request for the coming fiscal year would encounter little difficulty when it underwent legislative consideration. But the congressional critics of the New Look, especially those in the Senate, chose 1956 as the year to make a full-scale attack on the administration's defense program. That year saw the great debate over air power, with several of the administration's critics claiming that Eisenhower and Wilson had endangered national security by failing to request adequate funding for the Air Force. With Secretary Wilson as its chief spokesman, the administration maintained that its requests were sufficient and that any additional appropriations were both unnecessary and fiscally irresponsible. On that issue, then, the political debate was joined.

Actually a major disagreement between the administration and its opponents over the issue of national defense had been brewing for some time. In 1953 and 1954, criticism of the Eisenhower-Wilson defense program made headlines in national publications, but the proposed revisions in the New Look experienced parliamentary setbacks in a Republican-controlled Congress. While the Democrats regained control of Congress with their electoral victory in the 1954 midterm elections, they were unable to present an acceptable alternative to the New Look in 1955. By 1956, however, leading Democrats such as Richard Russell, Stuart Symington, and Henry Jackson had marshaled sufficient political strength to challenge the administration. Outspoken critics of the New Look, these senators also believed that Wilson's performance as secretary of defense left much to be desired. Furthermore, 1956 was a presidential election year, and several leading Democrats positioned themselves for a run at their party's nomination. After his heart attack, Eisenhower had slowed his presidential pace considerably, leaving many to wonder if he would seek a second term. If he did, his reelection seemed certain. With the nation enjoying renewed prosperity and a temporary relaxation in the international tensions of the Cold War, the president enjoyed widespread popularity. Not many issues were available to the Democrats to use against this popular chief executive, but the most plausible one appeared to be the administrations' tightfisted approach to spending, especially for national defense.

But in order to exploit the defense issue, the Democrats needed public dissent from the New Look by the nation's military leaders. For three years, the administration had profited from the general public sentiment that "if Ike doesn't know what the military needs, who does?"[2] Thus, the critics of Eisenhower and Wilson required strong support from some respected military men in order to validate their claim that their alternative to the New Look was more acceptable than the administration's policy. By 1956, certain segments of the armed services were indeed ready to demonstrate their hostility to the New Look. Some officers had even begun stating their independent cases to sympathetic congressmen and reporters. Of the leadership of the three major service branches, that of the Army was the most disheartened. Ever since the end of the Korean War, the Army had watched in dismay as the administration reduced its manpower and appropriation levels. Anxious to speak out, the proponents of a larger Army were nevertheless reluctant to do so. With a West Point graduate in

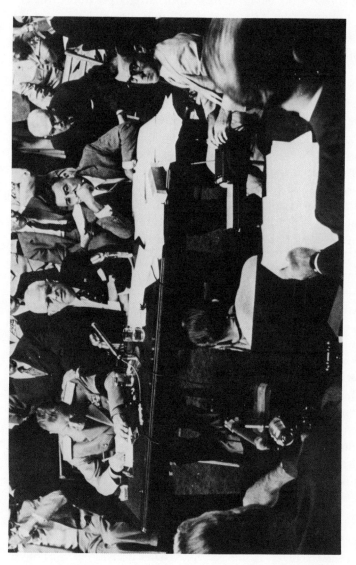

The Senate hearings in April 1956 revealed distinct differences of opinion between some senators and the administration. Wilson is responding to a question from Senator Stuart Symington, chairman of the air power subcommittee.

By permission of the Wilson Archives

the White House who never looked approvingly on public dissent from stated policies, the Army leadership understandably feared the repercussions of a direct break with Eisenhower.

Watching the gradual decline in the Army's capability was especially painful for Army Chief of Staff General Matthew B. Ridgway. Between 1953 and 1955, Ridgway had advocated a greater strategic role for the Army. But under Admiral Radford's leadership, the Joint Chiefs of Staff continued to adhere publicly to the New Look, with its commitment to air and sea power. Ridgway resigned after one disappointing term in the summer of 1955, convinced that the administration overemphasized the air power component at the expense of the ground forces. Upon his resignation, the general made a vigorous critique of the New Look in his final report to Wilson.[3]

Concerned that a full disclosure of Ridgway's remarks would undermine the New Look at a time when it was being considered by Congress, Wilson classified the report, intending to release it later. A young Army staff officer in the Pentagon smuggled the document from departmental files and gave it to the press, however.[4] The resulting furor over Ridgway's critique of the New Look focused public attention squarely upon Wilson, who was not pleased with this development. Although he had not discouraged Ridgway from making his views known, he had insisted upon a modicum of support for the administration policy once final decisions were made about it.

When General Maxwell D. Taylor was summoned to Washington to be questioned as Ridgway's possible successor, Eisenhower and Wilson explained to him the necessity of public support for the New Look. Taylor, who shared Ridgway's views about military strategy but who also wanted to be army chief of staff, took some offense at the interrogation by his civilian superiors. As he later recalled in his memoirs:

[Wilson] began to cross-examine me on my readiness to carry out civilian orders even when contrary to my own views. After thirty-seven years of service without evidence of insubordination, I had no difficulty of conscience in reassuring him, but I must say I was surprised to be put through such a loyalty test. Hence I had no hesitancy in assuring President Eisenhower, Secretary of Defense Wilson and other senior service officials in Washington who probed my views before my departure that I was quite prepared to live with a defensive strategy and not kick against the pricks.[5]

Eventually appointed to serve as army chief of staff, Taylor did little to help the administration in its relations with the Army. Author of a staff paper entitled "A National Military Policy," Taylor became the advocate of a theory of defense called "Flexible Response." The plan called for a substantial standing army, capable of fighting so-called brushfire wars and guerrilla insurgencies. New Look strategy, of course, provided that America's allies should carry the major combat responsibilities in such instances; American troops should not fight other people's wars.

The Navy was not as suspicious of the New Look as the Army. Although the administration's strategy offended some traditionalists in the Navy, the branch as a whole supported the overall policy.[6] The service's responsibilities and appropriations had increased somewhat under the New Look. Furthermore, Admiral Radford's presence as the chairman of the JCS insured the Navy a strong voice in military decision making.

As for the Air Force, its role in the national defense posture had increased dramatically since World War II, and by 1956, its budget was twice that of the Army. Increasingly influential on Capitol Hill, the service jealously guarded its newly won political strength, not wishing to have its position challenged by the other services. Although its strategic power was unmatched by any other force in the world, the Air Force continued to press for larger appropriations, regarding the administration's budget requests as "adequate, austere, and meeting minimum . . . requirements."[7] Furthermore, numerous congressmen and senators supported the Air Force during the 1950s. As a former secretary of the air force, Symington was knowledgeable about the service's requirements. With the emergence of what later became known as the military-industrial complex, legislators sought the favor of the Air Force for large defense contracts which meant jobs and votes in their home districts. If challenged, the service defended its political power through a well-orchestrated public relations effort.

By early 1956, the potential existed for an alliance between the administration's opposition in Congress, who sought to make political capital from an attack on the administration's defense program, and its critics in the military, who wanted a larger congressional appropriation for their respective services. When Wilson presented the fiscal year 1957 defense program to Congress in January 1956, he found a spate of resistance awaiting it.

During January and February, the secretary explained the third New Look budget to the armed services committees in both houses of Congress. In a prepared statement given before the Senate Armed Services Committee on 12 January, Wilson listed the administration's requests for each service. Requests for the Navy showed a small increase over the previous year, with the additional funding earmarked for the aircraft carrier component. The Army, however, incurred a loss in appropriations and a virtual freeze on its troop strength. Wilson revealed that the Air Force would continue its scheduled buildup to 137 wings and that the Pentagon intended to speed up production of the B-52 heavy bomber. This defense program, in terms both of its suggested manpower levels and of its budgetary requests, struck the Democratic leadership as highly inadequate. Symington and Jackson had argued for three years that the Republicans were more concerned with economic than military considerations in their defense planning. In their estimation, the administration's latest program validated that charge. Furthermore, the Army was openly criticizing "massive retaliation" and suggesting that a doctrine of "measured retaliation" suited the national interest better.[8]

Wilson faced a difficult situation. Symington, a presidential aspirant, almost certainly intended to renew his previous charge that the Soviets were overtaking the United States in total air strength. Opposition to the New Look showed signs of developing among certain segments of the press. An unhappy military might choose such a time for public criticism of existing policy. All that Wilson's opposition lacked was a headline event upon which to focus their dissatisfaction. In mid-January, however, such an event occurred, when the *Saturday Evening Post,* one of the nation's most popular and widely circulated magazines, began publication of six consecutive weekly excerpts from General Ridgway's memoirs, *Soldier.* The first two segments contained criticisms of the New Look, of Wilson's performance as secretary of defense, and of the administration's decision to emphasize

"Not in the Corridors, Dammit!"

From *Herblock's Special for Today* (Simon & Schuster, 1958)

air power instead of ground forces in its military planning. For the most part, Ridgway's remarks were reasonable. As a former Army officer, he presented alternatives to existing military policy; as a private citizen, he had every right to do so.

Yet the memoirs contained some elements which Wilson would have disputed, especially Ridgway's tone of alarm. Ridgway offered an image of himself as the solitary soldier who, appalled at the folly of his civilian superiors, patriotically chose his own wiser course to save the nation from imminent disaster. The excerpt published 28 January, entitled "Keep the Army out of Politics," illustrated that theme, as well as Ridgway's personal distaste for Wilson. Ridgway questioned Wilson's qualifications as the secretary of defense, portraying him as a man too concerned with politics to make positive military policy.

> From [Wilson's] office stemmed many suggestions that I take actions, which had I done so, would have seriously impaired the Army's capability to accomplish its missions and would have weakened esprit, which are the basic strengths of any military organization.... After each exchange of views, I came away convinced that either the Secretary was a man who operated on a level of genius so high that I could not grasp his meaning or that considerations beyond the ken of a soldier's logic were influencing his thinking.

Ridgway, in criticizing the Eisenhower administration's approach to formulating military policy, also warned against concentrating too much power in the hands of the civilian leadership of the Defense Department. "I think the tendency, which was manifest many times during my tenure as Chief of Staff, of civilian secretaries making military decisions on a basis of political considerations constitutes a danger to this country."[9]

Ridgway's implication was clear: Wilson placed a higher value on political and economic factors than on military considerations when he made the major decisions on defense policy. Ridgway's charge echoed those of the New Look's critics, and his distinguished reputation gave such claims a greater credibility. Furthermore, the *Post* articles coincided, almost to the week, with Wilson's presentation of the Pentagon budget to Congress. Senate Democrats gleefully grabbed at Ridgway's allegations, while the Washington press corps once more called upon Wilson to account for the general's remarks.

"Amazing"

Copyright 1956 by Herblock in the *Washington Post*

On 17 January, Wilson held a press conference to discuss the issues raised in Ridgway's article. Although the *Post* was not due to appear on the newsstands for almost a week, reporters had digested material from the advance copies and were prepared to question the secretary of defense about his relationship with the former army chief of staff. Specifically, the press asked if Wilson had quarreled with Ridgway or pressured him into agreement on matters of defense policy. Wilson answered no to both questions. He had not pressured any of the Joint Chiefs into silence on matters of defense policy. One of his replies demonstrated that Wilson felt no animosity toward Ridgway.

> I have no quarrel with General Ridgway and I am sure he is a dedicated officer that has done a great deal for his country, and I don't want to really comment on specific parts of the article. All the articles were submitted for security review and not a single request for deletions was made.
> I don't recall any such business [pressure], but of course, I do talk to the men about it and I don't expect any of my associates to polish the apple by seeming to agree with me when in their hearts they don't.[10]

Eisenhower also chose to reply to Ridgway's charges. In a statement released by Press Secretary James Hagerty on 19 January, the president indicated that he "never allowed politics to interfere with military considerations and that he had to make decisions based on the best advice."[11] The mildness of Eisenhower's statement concealed the extreme displeasure which he privately felt toward Ridgway. The administration wanted the JCS to take a corporate view of military decision making rather than to fall back into the dissension and wrangling that had occurred during the Truman years. Later in 1956, Eisenhower went so far as to inform Radford that he was considering requesting a new oath for the Pentagon's military and civilian officials, preferably one which forbade the disclosure of security information by retired officers or civilian officials no longer working at the Defense Department.[12]

Nevertheless, Ridgway's literary salvos at the administration constituted such potent political ammunition that the Democrats could scarcely afford to pass them up. Symington and Senator Estes Kefauver of Tennessee, both potential presidential candidates, immediately expressed their approval of the general's remarks, and suggested that Congress should examine the New Look in greater detail. Symington even offered to chair such an investigation.[13] Not wanting to be outdone, Kefauver called "for a thorough probe of the Defense Department." Ridgway "knows his business," the senator stated, and "it is wonderful for the country to have him speak up."[14] Other Democrats, including Henry Jackson, appeared on weekly news broadcasts to offer more criticism of the New Look.

In an effort to present the administration's case before a potentially confused public, Wilson called another news conference on 1 February, in which he stated his opinion of any imminent congressional investigation of the administration's defense program: "I am sympathetic with the great responsibilities that the Congressmen and Senators have to carry out their duties to their country. Any information that they need to do that, [they will receive] promptly. I do wish that some folks would get away from the theory that [the Pentagon] is made up of brass, bunglers, and bureaucrats because that is not what it is."[15] But, like January, February proved to be a month of problems for the secretary of defense. Late in the month, Trevor Gardner, the assistant secretary of the air force for research and development, resigned after a dispute with Wilson about the funding level for his area. Gardner left government service with a stinging rebuke of administration defense policy and the startling announcement that the United States faced the possibility of losing its air superiority over the Soviet Union.[16] On 24 February, Senate Armed Services Committee Chairman Russell authorized Symington to proceed with an investigation of the entire air power program. The subsequent Symington hearings added a new element to the debate over military spending.

In spite of the reversals which it seemed to have suffered in the first two months of 1956 regarding the defense program, the administration steadfastly continued to defend its policy. Throughout March, April, and May, Wilson used congressional hearings, press conferences, and public speeches in an effort to bolster popular support for the administration's military program.

On 6 March, the secretary met the air power issue head-on in a news conference with the Washington press. Asked if the Soviets were in a position to overtake the United States in terms of air strength, Wilson replied that the "Russians were probably building at a faster rate than the United States, but that's expected." Even so, he insisted that the combined air strength of the United States and its allies, including the Air Force and the air components of the Army, Navy, and Air Reserve, greatly exceeded that of the Communist bloc. When queried about his reaction to the scheduled Symington hearings, Wilson had difficulty suppressing his distaste for the opposition's tactics. The secretary believed that partisan political attacks on the defense program produced very few positive results and that he considered the coming hearings to be politically inspired. Insisting that the Pentagon's intelligence sources continued to report that American air power exceeded the Soviet Union's, Wilson now argued that a new investigation would turn up little in the way of new information. As for Symington himself, the secretary hoped that "he finds out that he doesn't know as much as he thinks he knows now." Wilson ended the news conference by suggesting that discussions of military power would not necessarily improve the troubled international situation. Warning against an overemphasis on military power as a curative for the tensions of the Cold War, he pointed out "that military power alone is not going to solve the world's problems and bring about a condition of peace. Some other things need to be done and that is why I am a little reluctant to join up in a demand for bigger and bigger Armies, Navies and Air Forces, bigger bombs, more bombs and all that kind of business."[17]

During March, the secretary also made two appearances before congressional committees to defend the administration's military program. On 13 March, he testified before the Senate Armed Services Committee and argued for the current proposals. The Eisenhower administration had brought stability to defense programming after a long period of "feast and famine," Wilson maintained. Although the American Air Force possessed a "vast capability," he warned against the attempt to get into a "numbers game" with the Soviets and try to match them plane for plane. Nevertheless, his testimony failed to convince the administration's critics. Before adjournment, Senator Russell recommended an additional $1.5 billion appropriation for the Air Force.[18] On 29 March, Wilson appeared before the House Appropriations Committee. This meeting proved equally frustrating, as the administration's critics continued to repeat the same charges. Furthermore, testimony by individual members of the JCS demonstrated that Wilson had been unable to reduce interservice tensions. General Taylor stated that while he "supported" the administration program, he felt that the Army needed additional personnel. Twining implied that the Russians would soon overtake the United States in numbers of aircraft unless Congress provided more money.[19] The hearings closed with committee Democrats issuing a general critique of the administration's defense policy.

Faced with mounting criticism, the administration decided to seek a compromise with its foes. The Symington hearings, which promised to be the first full review of American air power since the end of World War II, were slated to open on 16 April. During March and early April, the administration worked on a proposal for a supplemental increase to the defense budget for funds to be used mainly for modernization of the Air Force. The first estimate given to Wilson by the Joint Chiefs called for a supplement in the range of $4–6 billion. Eisenhower considered that figure unacceptable, and Wilson eventually reduced it to $547 million. Aware of Ridgway's earlier dissent, the president instructed Wilson that he expected no public disagreement from the Joint Chiefs over the size of the supplement.[20] In another action related to the supplemental increase in defense spending, Wilson announced the appointment of E. V. Murphree, the head of Esso Research and Engineering, as Gardner's successor as the official in charge of missile production. The administration hoped that both actions would serve to appease those of its critics who wanted substantial increases in funding for the Air Force as well as "single management" of the research and development effort in the ballistic missiles field.[21]

The administration then waited throughout April, as the various committees in Congress considered the issues involved in the national defense program. In early May, Wilson again journeyed to Capitol Hill. On 8 May, he made an important appearance before the Subcommittee on Defense Appropriations of the Senate Appropriations Committee. In a well-organized opening statement, the secretary dealt with the defense issues confronting the nation. He said in part:

During the past few months, there has been a great deal of public discussion concerning our defense needs. Statements have been made that the Soviets are ahead of the United States in this or that particular area—that they are building more airplanes or more submarines or more missiles than the United States. Some proponents of ballistic missiles urge that the United States increase its efforts in this field . . . others that we match the Russians plane for plane or ship for ship.

We could make perhaps the greatest mistake if we were to attempt to match the U.S.S.R. division for division or man for man. To do so would ignore the difference between our geographic positions and more importantly would ignore the great contributions which can be made by our allies in this area.

Let us turn now to the subject of airpower. You are all familiar with the almost daily stories alleging that the U.S.S.R. is far outstripping the United States in terms of airpower. That is not so.

When I speak of airpower, I include in that term the total strength of our Air Force, not a selected part of it, the total strength of the Navy, the Marine Corps, the Army, the Air National Guard and Air Reserve Units of all our services, plus the civilian production capability and the airpower of our allies.[22]

When the committee members began their questioning, their primary concern was the air power issue, although neither Wilson nor the committee members offered much in the way of new information. Basically, the interrogation ground down to a test of wills, with committee Democrats attacking the administration's requests as insufficient and Wilson defending them. The secretary did mention, however, that the total value of any defense program depended on the willingness of its citizens to pay, and be taxed, for its cost. If Congress insisted on raising the appropriations, it should also increase taxes to pay for them.[23]

By mid-May, the administration and the Democratic Congress seemed to be deadlocked over the issue of military spending for the upcoming fiscal year. Sentiment in Congress leaned toward increasing the supplemental appropriation for the Air Force, with the Army and Navy funded at the administration's suggested levels. The House and the Senate disagreed, however, on the desirable amount for the Air Force. Democratic congressmen generally favored a small increase, in the neighborhood of $200–400 million, while the administration's critics in the Senate advocated an increase of more than $1 billion. But the administration appeared equally determined to hold the line on higher defense costs. In 1955, Eisenhower had successfully steered the second New Look through an opposition Congress. Another test of wills would certainly not be new. Wilson continued

'Massive Retaliation'

By permission of *The Washington Star*

steadfastly to defend the budget, indicating that he, too, was opposed to any substantially higher appropriation. With the potential for stalemate increasing, the executive and legislature looked for a compromise which would enable each side to keep certain of its goals intact.

Congress scheduled full debate on the defense budget for early June. Wilson, of course, wanted the Pentagon to present a united front while that debate progressed, so as to avoid partisanship as much as possible. In late May, he attended Armed Forces Day festivities outside Washington, events which serve to underscore American military unity. One reporter covering Wilson, however, noticed that the secretary seemed unusually preoccupied. At one point, Wilson even remarked that several Army colonels had been leaking confidential staff papers and other classified documents to friendly newsmen during the previous week. This leak campaign, he noted, was causing "more trouble than we should have."²⁴ In truth, the Army's leaks were part of an elaborate campaign to raise its own public support while undermining Air Force power on Capitol Hill. Occurring when it did, the Army's action represented a last-ditch effort to sabotage the administration's defense program before it received congressional approval.

After becoming army chief of staff, Maxwell Taylor found himself under considerable pressure from several young officers who supported Ridgway's views. One of them, Colonel Donovan Yeuell, urged Taylor to take political advantage of the controversy which Ridgway's memoirs had created. Yeuell wanted Taylor to undertake a campaign to discredit the New Look before the Air Force's position became more entrenched on Capitol Hill. Taylor expressed some interest in Yeuell's idea, but he had a determined reluctance to make a public break with Wilson and Eisenhower unless he was assured that any such campaign could not be traced to the Army staff. Without Taylor's supervision, but with his knowledge, the colonels prepared to distribute anti-New Look position papers to Washington reporters and legislators. Yeuell contacted his brother-in-law, Wallace Carroll, the news editor of the *New York Times* Washington bureau, and asked him to be the recipient of these papers. Carroll agreed to serve as the Army's contact but only if he received assurances from the general staff that ranking Army officers supported this campaign. Shortly thereafter, Yeuell introduced Carroll to Lieutenant General Lyal C. Metheny, the officer who was to release the position papers to the press.²⁵

By early May, the *New York Times* began to publish parts of the position papers. One such paper, "A Decade of Insecurity through Global Air Power," was highly critical of the Air Force's strategic role, while advocating a newer and more vigorous role for the Army. Not to be outdone, Air Force staff officers soon began leaking memos critical of the Army's role to reporters who were generally sympathetic to the Air Force position. Open feuding between the two services began after Colonel Robert L. Scott, the Air Force information director, released a paper appropriately entitled "A Decade of Security through Global Air Power."[26] By the middle of May, the military affairs reporter for the *New York Times,* Anthony Leviero, wrote publicly on the latest round of interservice rivalry.[27]

Wilson remained fully aware of the hostility and suspicion between the Army and Air Force leadership. He was, however, away from Washington when Leviero's articles began appearing in the *Times.* After reading the press reports, Wilson decided that his toleration of the interservice feuding had ended. Leviero's articles made him furious, as had Ridgway's earlier parting-shot memoirs in the *Saturday Evening Post,* and he determined to resolve the issue even if it meant the forced resignation of several top-level military officers.[28]

On 21 May, Wilson assembled the service secretaries and members of the JCS before a Pentagon news conference for the purpose, as he put it, of "clarify[ing] this situation." Usually the secretary conducted his press conferences informally, but on this occasion, he read a prepared statement before answering any questions. The tone of his remarks showed his extreme displeasure.

Stories have appeared in the press over the weekend placing great emphasis on the differences among the military on how their roles should be carried out. Some of the documents that have been quoted in the press are staff papers that reflect the views of individuals who worked on them and not necessarily the approved policies of the services. As such differences and misunderstandings can become serious matters, I have asked the Service Secretaries and members of the Joint Chiefs of Staff to appear with me at this news conference to clarify this situation.

There will always be some differences of opinion with and between the services in connection with their military operations. Honest differences and reasonable competition will result in a stronger defense establishment. It is not good, however, to have these differences, some of which are set forth in confidential staff papers, aired on a basis of service partisanship without giving proper responsible officials the opportunity to weigh all the factors involved.

Current roles and missions have been determined by the Secretary of Defense upon the recommendations of the Joint Chiefs of Staff. The great advances in technology and development of revolutionary weapons require continual review. The Chairman and the JCS continually have this matter under review. Any re-assignment of roles and missions that may be required in the future among the services will be based on what is in the best interests of the country and must not be adversely influenced by the promotional activities of partisan service representatives.[29]

After questioning Wilson, the reporters immediately asked General Taylor for his explanation of the Army's role in the controversy. Taylor vacillated between a direct condemnation of the leaks ("I have taken the position of going along with and supporting the present budget for 1957 and there is no revolt in the Army"), to qualified support for the colonels ("I would not prejudge the case"), to his final disclaimer ("I am initiating an investigation"). Some of Taylor's responses demonstrated his unhappiness with the incident, such as his statement that he "would like to know who the colonels are."[30]

Wilson's intervention in the "leaked memo" campaign routed the Army's secret dissenters. The Army general staff prohibited Yeuell and the other colonels from coming to their offices. General William Westmoreland, Taylor's chief aide, became responsible for disciplining the offenders. Yeuell, whose files were emptied and burned, was reassigned to the Army War College and Metheny to a dreary post in Florida. Other participants in the rebellion received transfers to obscure posts away from Washington. The Army leadership never challenged Wilson again.[31]

But the secretary's handling of the Army's rebellion failed to impress the Air Force leadership. By assembling the members of the JCS at a press conference and defying them to oppose administration policy, Wilson hoped to serve notice that he wanted no further public challenges to the administration's stated defense objectives. Judging from subsequent events, the Air Force leadership interpreted Wilson's action only as a bureaucratic setback for the Army, and not as generally applicable to its own lobbying effort on Capitol Hill. At any rate, both LeMay and Twining continued to inform congressional committees that the administration's requests were austere and inadequate.[32]

While Wilson tried to reduce the interservice quarreling within the Pentagon, Symington conducted the first two phases of his hearings. Covering several stages, the subcommittee's investigation into American air power involved a review of American air strength since World War II, comparisons between estimates of American air power and that of the Soviets, and finally, Wilson's testimony as related to the group's overall findings.[33]

Essentially, Symington's probe sought to resolve one question: was the United States losing its strategic air strength to the Soviet Union? According to Symington, the Soviet Union was devoting more effort to the production of its Bison heavy bomber than the United States was to the production of its B-52. Furthermore, he warned that Soviet technology might soon make improvements in the Bison which would make it qualitatively superior to the B-52. Wilson steadfastly maintained that the American plane was superior and would remain so for years to come. But because of the sensitive nature of the subject, he declined to cite production statistics or other confidential data while the hearings remained open. He did, however, examine a report prepared by the subcommittee entitled "Present and Planned Strengths of the United States Air Force." Prepared as a result of the 16 April testimony by military leaders to Symington's subcommittee, this detailed document represented the committee's analysis of the existing air power situation.[34]

In early June, Congress began its debate on the defense budget for the upcoming fiscal year. Throughout 1956, the administration's Democratic opposition had been moving in the direction of appropriating more funds for the Air Force. Such action became an almost absolute certainty as Symington's hearings ran concurrently with the general debate.

The House moved first on the air power issue. On 9 June it authorized an additional $248 million for the Air Force, which would allow an increase in B-52 production from seventeen to twenty planes per month. The administration accepted the House's decision and instructed the Pentagon to follow through with the procurement directive.[35] The Senate, however, was thinking in much larger terms, considering increases of anywhere from $1.1 billion to $3.8 billion.

Certain Democratic senators apparently thought the Air Force's already large $15.7 billion budget was insufficient.[36] Wilson considered such proposals totally unwarranted. Future defense plans called for the development of guided missile systems which would eventually perform some of the functions of the B-52. To invest more money in a program which promised to become obsolescent made little sense strategically and even less economically.

On the weekend of 20 June, Wilson attended the annual Service Secretaries Conference at Quantico, Virginia. This event brought civilian and military officials together for an analysis of past and future trends in defense programming. On 21 June, Wilson held a news conference to discuss the latest developments in the air power controversy. It proved to be one of his most explosive conferences.

Wilson first announced that the Pentagon had recently increased B-52 production to the level requested by the Air Force. Turning to the political scene, the reporters asked Wilson whether he favored the Democratic proposal of authorizing an additional $1.2 billion for the Air Force or Senator Bridges's Republican-sponsored compromise of $500 million. The secretary replied that both were unnecessary. But, Wilson said, if the additional funds were appropriated, "I would look at it more like my bankers had insisted I had more credit in the bank than I needed."[37] In other words, he threatened to use the funds as a cash carry-over into the next fiscal year.

Wilson then digressed to relate some details about a recent trip to the Pacific where he had witnessed a nuclear test. After that, he answered a question pertaining to a recent British decision to reduce their defense expenditures. Charles Corddry of the United Press then shouted, "Yours [problems] are to stave off more money, aren't they?" The secretary candidly replied:

> I think that's a phony [issue]. . . . Well, maybe I shouldn't have said it, but the people of our country quite properly want to make sure we have a strong defense and we are taking care of the security of our nation, but when it comes to paying the taxes to do it, some people take a little different slant on that, and I would just like to see the people that vote for the expenditures . . . vote for the taxes to pay for [them].[38]

Wilson's statement illustrated his view of any supplemental appropriation. In the first place, he considered any increases unnecessary. But if Congress insisted on increasing the Air Force budget, it must also vote for the taxes to cover the increased cost. That would not happen, Wilson argued, because the increases could not stand analysis and served only political purposes.

Wilson's use of the word "phony" to describe the Senate's deliberations provoked an immediate uproar on Capitol Hill. A week of intense breast-beating ensued, with several Democrats calling for the secretary's resignation. Senator Henry Jackson's remarks in a speech on the Senate floor typify the criticism of Wilson.

> In my humble judgment—and I said this more than three years ago, he should no longer serve as Secretary of Defense.
> His latest comment has demonstrated his ability to keep his foot in his mouth most of the time. The rest of the time, he is trying desperately to take his foot out of his mouth.

Others soon joined in the condemnation, not wanting to be outdone by Jackson's remarks. Dennis Chavez (D.-N. Mex.) stated, "Wilson forgets he is not running General Motors"; Sam Ervin (D.-N.C.) complained, "The Secretary is more concerned about dollars than security"; and George Smathers (D.-Fla.) observed that Wilson "can make more errors than Mickey Mantle can make hits."[39]

But the most outspoken of Wilson's critics was Richard Russell. He complained that the secretary's "arrogance and vanity" were exceeded "only by his ineptness." The senator charged that Wilson "sought to intimidate" the armed services leadership from "fully expressing their opinions to, and advising with, the Congress on the all-important matter of national defense." Continuing his speech with the comment, Wilson needs "a short course in the American Constitution," Russell thus completed one of the most vigorous attacks yet on any of Eisenhower's cabinet members.[40]

The entire week was difficult for the secretary, especially since no Republicans came to his support in his latest clash with the Senate. On 26 June, the Bridges amendment (perhaps in retaliation for the "phony" remark) was defeated in the Senate, thereby dooming any chance for a compromise between the administration and its opposition on the Air Force budget.[41] On 28 June, the day immediately before Wilson's scheduled appearance before the Symington subcommittee, the Senate passed a $900 million supplement to the Air Force budget. There were, however, two bright spots for the secretary in an otherwise gloomy week. Some newspapers published editorials defending his position in the air power controversy and claiming that certain senators overreacted to the "phony" remark. An editorial in the 26 June *New York Daily News,* entitled "Oh, Let Charlie Talk!," typified the pro-Wilson sentiment. It read in part:

> Include us out, please, of the attacks on Defense Secretary Charles E. Wilson for having applied the word "phony" to the Congressional talk about hiking Air Force funds.
> Sure, Charlie acts like a bull in a China shop now and then. But he is an ace executive and has done an excellent Defense Department job up to now. We say let him stay there as long as he delivers results; and what's wrong with having it least one Cabinet officer who always says what he thinks?

Eisenhower also voiced his support for Wilson. Distressed by the Senate's action, he instructed the secretary to "lay it on the line" when he appeared before the Subcommittee on the Air Force.[42]

Wilson testified before the Symington subcommittee between 29 June and 3 July. Testimony released from those sessions indicated that little new ground was covered. Democratic members of the group maintained that additional funds were necessary to offset increased Russian capability. Wilson and the Republican members of the subcommittee asserted that the Democrats were overly pessimistic about American air strength and that the administration's estimates were reliable. The highlights of the hearings, then, involved several heated exchanges between Wilson and his Senate critics, exchanges which demonstrated the partisanship generated by the issue. On 29 June, Wilson defended the administration against Senator Jackson's charges that it overemphasized economic factors in the formulation of its defense program. The secretary pointed out that "it is always a question of priorities. No one can take the position that money is of no object, and it is endless."[43]

On 2 July, Ervin, Jackson, and Wilson argued repeatedly. Ervin characterized the administration's program as "one of reduce, curtail and postpone." That program, Ervin said, reminded him of "a man in my town who said, 'now, good boy, if you want to get along in this world, you just have to do without the things you have to have.'" The senator's storytelling proclivities apparently did not impress Wilson, however, who continued to maintain that the necessity for additional funds would not stand analysis, and, if appropriated, such funds would be used only in the most necessary area. On 3 July, Ervin impatiently snapped:

> It seems to me that the attitude of the Defense Department is like that of the old lady who went to a lawyer's office and asked for legal advice. She got up and started out. The lawyer said, "Wait a minute, you owe me $5." The old lady said, "What for?" He said, "For my advice." She said, "I ain't agwine to take it."
>
> And isn't that exactly what you are telling us, that you don't propose to take the advice of Congress on that matter. The Secretary is just like the old lady. He is keeping the money and not taking the legal advice on bombers.[44]

Ervin's questioning hardly appealed to Wilson, but Senator Jackson's was even more annoying. During the course of the hearings, Jackson had vainly attempted to force Wilson's agreement that the administration had erred in its budgetary estimates for the Air Force. But the secretary steadfastly defended the entire program. Finally, Jackson turned to Wilson's "phony" remark in a last effort to state his differences with the administration. For the next several minutes, the two men exchanged verbal blows, with Ervin and Symington attempting to interrupt their remarks.

Jackson: Do you feel that you owe an apology to Congress for having made it?
Wilson: I do not.
Jackson: You feel you do not owe an apology?
Wilson: I do not , and if you want to be technical about it, it would not be out of order for certain Senators to apologize to me.
Jackson: About what?
Wilson: Well, you are one of them.
Jackson: Well, that is fine. I just want to say this, Mr. Wilson, that the difficulties you have had with the Congress have stemmed from your own

statements and when not a single member of your own party stood up and defended you, I think that speaks for itself.

Ervin: Mr. Chairman, if I could inject a bit of personal philosophy around here at this point, I would just like to add that my personal experience has been that men very rarely regret saying too little . . .

Wilson: That is correct, sir, and I might tell you a story . . .

Symington: It becomes apparent that we won't finish . . .

Wilson: This is what the mama whale said to the baby calf. The mama whale said to her calf, "Son, always remember that it is only when you are blowing that you are liable to be harpooned."

Jackson: I think the public knows who has been doing a lot of blowing.[45]

With his anticipated exposé of administration failure degenerating into a partisan shouting match, Symington tried to restore some dignity to the hearings. Jackson, Ervin, and Wilson refrained from further argument, and the hearings resumed their course. But each side appeared spent by the year's ordeal and little of substance was accomplished. In closing the hearings, Symington charged that Wilson's remarks conflicted with those of the military, and he added that he supported the $900 million congressional supplement. Speaking for the minority, Saltonstall defended Wilson's testimony and commented that "honest differences of opinion" tended to cloud the complex issue of national defense. He refused to support the supplemental bill, preferring instead to place his confidence in the president's military judgment.[46]

But the fact remained that the Democrats scored a political victory over the administration in their passage of the final defense budget in 1956. The $34.7 billion total exceeded Eisenhower and Wilson's requests by over $500 million. In pure dollar terms, that figure was not drastically higher than the administration's original proposal. Yet it did represent the first time that Democrats in Congress had overruled Eisenhower and Wilson on the specifics of defense policy. The president did, however, sign the defense bill; he did not comment on it at the time.[47]

To Wilson the congressional supplement to the Air Force budget represented an unwise piece of legislation. Furthermore, the year's political struggle presented a picture to the nation of the legislative and executive branches fighting over what should ideally have been a

"Ezra, You Got Any Storage Bins You're Not Using?"

bipartisan issue. Even so, Wilson remained popular in the eyes of many Americans. The Long Island daily, *Newsday,* published an editorial entitled "Where's Charlie?" on 5 July, the day after Wilson finished his testimony before the Symington subcommittee. Complimentary to Wilson, this editorial analyzed the secretary's relationship with his Senate critics, and said in part:

> It is impossible for anyone who is not thoroughly informed, including with much secret information, to decide who is right about the B-52 question. But we do feel Wilson's manner is the root of more trouble than any real ineptitude as Secretary of Defense. Some of the biggest bobbles he has made have been tactless—but they did express the truth as he saw it. The Democrats who impugn his integrity or his devotion to his job are playing politics. They may disagree with the substance of what Wilson says and they certainly do disagree with his manner of saying it, but it seems to us that Wilson's candor is a refreshing breeze on the stuffy, gobbledygook-laden Washington scene.

Nevertheless, the partisan political strife took its toll on Wilson. Since 1953, he had worked full time on the problems of administering the Pentagon, while also keeping a recalcitrant military in line and serving as the administration's defense spokesman before a hostile Congress. The last role was perhaps the most difficult, as Wilson seemed to be the opposition's favorite target. Every so often in the autumn months of 1956, rumors circulated that Wilson intended to resign his post after the presidential election. Wilson hinted at it himself in late October, when he made an appearance on the weekly news broadcast, "Face the Nation." Asked by James Shepley of Time-Life, Inc. if he intended to remain in a second Eisenhower administration, Wilson replied:

> When I took the job on, I made no time commitment and I haven't established any in my mind yet. . . . I know that—the time will come when I think the job should be turned over to someone else. I've had it, I guess, now twice as long as any of my four predecessors, and I knew them all four quite well.[48]

Eisenhower's victory in 1956 assured the continuation of the administration's defense objectives, however. Wilson stayed at the Pentagon for almost the entire first year of Eisenhower's second term. Buoyed by a Pentagon audit showing that the Air Force appropriation had

"I Can Do It for You Wholesale"

From *Herblock's Special for Today* (Simon & Schuster, 1958)

been excessive by $900 million in the 1957 fiscal year, the secretary was soon hard at work on the formulation of another military program.[49] Much of the supplemental appropriation was later earmarked for use in the guided missile program. And being Charles E. Wilson, he managed to stir up another round of controversy with the Senate in the early months of 1957.

8

Draft-dodgers and Dunghills:
Controversy over the National Guard

As secretary of defense, Charles E. Wilson often encountered
political trouble when he used offhand or sometimes flippant
statements to explain his views on official policy. In four-and-a-half
years at the Pentagon, Wilson had never tried to confuse the press or
the public with ambiguous language, but his bluntness and candor
occasionally seemed out of place in official Washington. Wilson's style
and manner, of course, had different effects on different people.
Some of his political critics regarded his apparent personal simplicity
as evidence of a second-rate mind and temperament. Even some of
the members of the administration, such as Emmett John Hughes,
were astonished at times by Wilson's apparent lack of political sophis-
tication.[1] The press corps, however, knew the secretary as one of the
rare accessible government officials who held regular news conferences.[2] Similarly, he appeared to have good working relations with
subordinates in the Pentagon. The *New York Times* of 24 February
1957 reported one of Wilson's associates as saying, "Wilson was one of
the greatest guys I ever worked with. Most bosses want you to come in,
sit down, say what you've got to say and get out. He wants you to sit
back, relax and have a thorough visit."

During the early months of 1957, Wilson needed the full reservoir
of trust which he had developed over the previous four years. While
most Washington observers expected him to leave the cabinet some-
time during the year, the secretary had announced his intention to
participate in the presentation of the fiscal year 1958 defense budget
before Congress. Included in the proposed military program was a

change in the national reserve program. Wilson had agreed with an earlier Army directive that all National Guard recruits should have six months of basic training, the same as the recruits in the other reserve forces. It was Wilson's remarks about the proposed change in the status of the National Guard which provided some interesting political fireworks during January and February and thrust the secretary into the limelight once again.

Congress had originally approved the administration's National Reserve Plan (NRP) during the summer of 1955, thereby enabling the administration to achieve two of its defense objectives: retaining sufficient trained forces for mobilization in the event of war and reducing the cost of a large standing military establishment. Participation in the reserve program would require an initial six-month period of basic training for each new enlistee.[3] Another provision of the NRP stipulated that the reserve forces would be divided into "ready" and "standby" categories. The Ready Reserve was to be a trained and organized force available for general mobilization and included the National Guard. By contrast, the Standby Reserve was essentially a manpower pool from which individuals could be called for any additional military service.

Both during and after the debate over its enactment, the NRP encountered considerable opposition. It was especially unpopular with the National Guard Association (NGA), the political and administrative arm of the National Guard. The NGA did not favor the six-month training program required of reserve forces by the administration's program. One of the National Guard's major recruiting and enlistment incentives lay in the provision that its enlistees needed only to attend weekly drills and one two-week summer encampment to fulfill their training requirement. A guardsman was thus able, over the course of several years, to satisfy his military obligation while remaining at home and not undergoing the basic training required of other reservists. Furthermore, any enlistee was ineligible for the draft provided he continued his preparation with the National Guard. For obvious reasons, the NGA believed that any change in the training requirements for guardsmen, especially if these requirements placed the National Guard on a level with the other reserve forces, would damage its recruiting and enlistment program.[4]

The NGA's political strength was evident in 1955 when it lobbied effectively against the National Reserve Plan and managed to persuade Congress to exempt guardsmen from the six-month training requirement.[5] Indeed, the NGA was one of the most effective lobbies operating in Washington. Its legislative staff included Ellard Walsh, president of the NGA, and Brigadier General Mark H. Galusha, formerly a legislative assistant with the Senate Armed Services Committee. Several influential senators were former guardsmen, including Theodore F. Green (D.-R.I.), Barry Goldwater (R.-Ariz.), and Edward Martin (R.-Pa.). Adding to the National Guard's political power was the fact that many state governors vigorously supported the service's activities. Membership in the National Guard numbered over 440,000 officers and recruits, and, as this sizable group's representative, the NGA sought to protect the organization from any intrusions upon its operation, either by the various branches of the armed services or by the Department of Defense.

In early 1957, Wilson decided to make some changes in the reserve program. Specifically, he intended to increase the number of Standby Reserve forces and finance the move by reducing the size of the National Guard. Furthermore, acting on the Army's advice, Wilson issued a directive that, as of 1 April 1957, all National Guard recruits would be required to undergo the six-month training program required of other reservists.

On 28 January, the secretary appeared before the House Armed Services Committee to explain the administration's policy regarding the reserve program. He told the committee that both he and President Eisenhower believed that the National Guard's present training program was inadequate and new recruits needed at least six months of military preparation. Furthermore, Wilson indicated that the National Guard had not cooperated fully in the reserve program and that the new directive would allow the Defense Department to apply a uniform standard for all reserve units. But the secretary almost ruined his presentation when he remarked, "The Guard was a sort of scandal during the Korean War, a draft-dodging business. A boy 17 to 18½ could enlist in the National Guard and not be drafted to fight in Korea."[6] Although National Guard recruits who enlisted during the Korean War were not technically "draft-dodgers," considerable public resentment had been aroused. Guardsmen, many with little or no previous military experience, had remained in the United States while over 600,000 veterans of World War II were recalled to active front-line service in Korea.[7] Many Americans felt that thousands of young men had joined the National Guard in order to escape combat duty.

At any rate, an immediate outcry resulted when Wilson's remarks were published. General Walsh called Wilson's statement a "damn lie. None of these young men is a draft-dodger." State National Guard commanders followed Walsh's criticism of Wilson with attacks of their own. George Moran, adjutant general of the Michigan National Guard, claimed to be "dumbfounded that the Secretary of Defense could make such a statement." Major General Milton Reckord, commander of the Maryland unit and influential in the NGA, charged that Wilson's statement was "a deliberate, despicable falsehood." Public reaction to Wilson's remark was also hostile. After questioning from the press, Defense Department officials revealed that the Pentagon had received numerous telephone calls and telegrams, running fifteen to one against the secretary.[8]

Congressional sentiment also ran strongly against the secretary. In the House, Indiana Republican William G. Bray, himself a former guardsman, announced, "Wilson's testimony demonstrated that the Defense Department was entirely unsympathetic to a real Reserve program." Representative Jack Brooks, Democrat from Texas, promised that his armed services subcommittee would want a thorough explanation from Wilson. In similar fashion, most of Wilson's long-time critics in the Senate were quick to condemn his remarks. Between 29 January and 3 February, several Democrats kept up a constant stream of criticism of him. Lyndon B. Johnson claimed that the secretary's statements "cast a cloud upon all Americans who have served in the National Guard." Estes Kefauver flatly called for Wilson's resignation.[9] Other senators, including Russell Long, Dennis Chavez, John Stennis, and William Fulbright, read condemnations of Wilson's statement into the *Congressional Record* and inserted complimentary remarks about their own state National Guard units.[10]

Furthermore, no Republican senator chose to defend Wilson. Although most GOP senators were not as critical as Wayne Morse, who declared that "Wilson was never qualified for the job and he is not

"The Trouble With You, Charlie, Is That You Say What You Think"

now," many echoed the view of George Aiken of Vermont, who said, "The Secretary has lost a great deal of confidence among those with whom he has to work."[11] With the press joining in the criticism of the secretary, Washington speculated as to Wilson's future in the administration, if indeed he still had one.

On 29 January, the day after his "draft-dodger" remark, Wilson went to the White House for a conference with Eisenhower. Afterward he met informally with waiting newsmen to discuss the National Guard controversy. Attempting to clarify the meaning of his previous statement, the secretary explained:

> If anybody thinks I am against the National Guard, of course they are wrong. I'm trying to get the National Guard efficient and trained. I am told that more than 80% of the National Guard [units] had no prior military training. That means they are not a very well-trained outfit that can be depended upon. We are spending a good many hundreds of millions of dollars on the National Guard and if they cannot be depended upon, the expense is not justified. The people who are trying to perpetuate the inefficiency are doing the Guard damage.[12]

Because it was raining, Wilson tried to hurry the meeting along. He maintained that his statement about the National Guard was not discussed during the conference. Then what did the discussion involve?, asked one reporter. The secretary stated curtly, "This is not my dunghill. Anything to be announced, somebody else [at the White House] ought to announce it." His apparent characterization of the White House as a "dunghill" brought Wilson some additional headlines in the evening newspapers.[13]

On 30 January, Eisenhower held a formal press conference. As expected, Wilson's "draft-dodger" statement brought inquiries from the reporters. William A. Lawrence of the *New York Times* asked the president if he shared Wilson's thinking concerning the National Guard situation. Cautiously, Eisenhower replied:

> Well, of course, you know better, really, than that—I don't. [The National Guard] is never going to be the kind of force we need, until we give these recruits at least six months of good, hard, basic training.
>
> Now that is correct, and I am talking about the training of the Guard, and I am not pointing a finger at anyone, and I am sure Secretary Wilson wasn't. He was short-cutting and making a very, I think, unwise statement.

King of the Hill

By permission of *Newsday*

Eisenhower was disappointed in Wilson's remarks, although he believed National Guard enlistees needed additional training. Trying to take some of the pressure off Wilson, however, the president met with four National Guard officers on 4 February and assured them that he would not allow the Guard "to be destroyed or reduced materially in strength."[14] But the secretary, thoroughly denounced in Congress, criticized by the press, and then admonished by Eisenhower, seemed to have suffered an irreparable political setback.

In spite of the criticism, from both his opponents and the president, Wilson intended to ask Congress to approve the administration's reserve program, including the six-month training requirement for guardsmen. He had no desire either to resign or be forced from office. On 1 February, he outlined his thoughts on the National Guard controversy by issuing a public statement from his office.

While he "meant no reflection on any individual young men," the secretary insisted that the National Guard's training program was woefully inadequate. Under his direction, the Defense Department intended to improve that program.

The secretary's statement coincided with a timely although unplanned event on 31 January. Jessie Wilson, the secretary's wife for forty-five years, had telephoned a Washington reporter whom she knew and expressed her resentment of Eisenhower's description of Wilson's remark as "unwise." Upset that the president refused to defend her husband publicly, Mrs. Wilson said that she was urging Wilson to quit the cabinet. In a story printed by the *Washington Post*, Mrs. Wilson reportedly said:

> I know the President means to be fair but once in awhile a slap on the back would be helpful to one who is doing a good job. I know he [Wilson] speaks bluntly, but it takes courage to do it. . . . I know he is unpredictable, but he is interesting. It is easy to criticize, but maybe some people would have a different view if they were working seven days a week at a job like he has. I've stood back and listened to criticism until I'm disgusted of it. You reach a point sometimes and this was it.[15]

Mrs. Wilson was under some strain in Washington, having recently been released from the hospital after treatment for ulcers. Normally a healthy person, she had developed the condition while Wilson was serving as secretary of defense. By all accounts the Wilsons and their six children were a close family that, in spite of their wealth, had informal tastes and often seemed out of place in protocol-minded Washington. For example, the Wilsons refused the government transportation at their disposal, and patrons of the Washington National Airport were sometimes surprised to see them waiting in line at the Eastern Airlines desk for tickets for their visits to Michigan. For Mrs. Wilson, life in Washington seemed chiefly to involve her husband's work, for she often recalled bringing him a fresh change of clothes after he had worked what he called "the night shift" at the Pentagon.[16]

Mrs. Wilson's telephone call raised an immediate uproar in Washington. While conceding that the secretary should not have said "dunghill" in his recent meeting with the press, by the defense of her husband Jessie Wilson raised the level of political interest in Washington considerably. Within days, a steady stream of letters and telegrams supporting Wilson poured into the Pentagon. A number of letters critical of the president for failing to support Wilson's testimony were sent to Eisenhower. Sherman Adams, the chief White House assistant, then referred these letters to the Pentagon for Wilson's review. Two themes tended to recur in them. First, most of the correspondents agreed with Wilson that the National Guard was not a well-trained force. Second, the writers congratulated the secretary for his candor and lamented that few public officials were as outspoken in their opinions.[17]

Two of the letters which came to Wilson's attention supported his position particularly forcefully. In a sharply worded critique of the National Guard's political activities, James T. Williams, former editor of the *Boston Evening Transcript,* wrote:

During my active years as a journalist, the National Guard and its evil ally—the Adjutant Generals Association—were two of the most powerful, insidious and contemptible lobbies operating in the Federal City. They are chiefly to blame, as I believe, for the defeat of all legislation for Universal Military Training, so earnestly urged by such statesmen as Theodore Roosevelt, Elihu Root, Leonard Wood, Henry L. Stimson and George Catlett Marshall.

In the other letter, Ernest Dale, a professor at the Graduate School of Business and Public Administration of Cornell University, commented on the National Guard's military limitations and congratulated Wilson for speaking out against them.

I whole-heartedly support the stand which you took on the National Guard. It was high time that somebody exposed its shortcomings. I touched on the subject once with General Eisenhower when he was president at Columbia and I believe he is in sympathy with the point I am making.

This is a major reason why I am writing to ask that you will seriously consider to remain in the Administration—we could ill afford to do without a man like yourself.[18]

Other letters covered a wide range of topics. Some writers sent clippings from their local newspapers which showed the NGA's recruiting promotions.[19] David K. Jameson, a former sergeant in the Texas National Guard, told the secretary that his opinion was "so right. Many guys did join the National Guard to avoid the draft." Mrs. G. Fohlen of Chatham, New York, wrote, "We do not feel that Secretary Wilson has in any way impaired his ability to carry out his duties. He is *blunt*, he is *honest*, he is doing a good job. Expressing an opinion honestly seems to be a thing to fear. As soon as a man is truthful, a handful of Senators want him fired."[20]

By 2 February, Wilson and Eisenhower apparently had decided to alter the course of the controversy. When the furor over the "draft-dodging" remark subsided, Wilson began seeking congressional support for the Pentagon's training directive. Even though several senators had previously spoken harshly about Wilson's description of the National Guard's training program, a good number of them fundamentally agreed that recruits needed additional preparation. There was a fair possibility that Congress might enact some acceptable legislation to improve the Guard. Moreover, with public opinion now supporting Wilson, several influential Republican senators gave him a vote of confidence. Saltonstall hoped that "Mr. Wilson stays in the Pentagon for at least the remainder of the present session of Congress." Goldwater felt that the secretary had "really done a wonderful job," and Francis Case of South Dakota, the sponsor of the existing legislation involving the National Guard, indicated that Wilson should remain at his job.[21]

Throughout February, the administration continued to press publicly for its proposal to correct the National Guard training program. On 3 February, General Taylor appeared on a television interview and stated his belief that the Guard was not sufficiently prepared to perform "those indispensable duties" required of it. On 7 February, Senator Martin, a former major general in the Pennsylvania National Guard, joined Senators Case and Chavez in sponsoring a bill authorizing a new training program.[22] The Case-Chavez-Martin proposal, Senate Bill 1017, provided a National Guard recruit with the option of completing his training in one of two specified ways. He could participate in the six-month program required of other reservists or attend two eleven-week drills in consecutive summers. If approved, the bill was scheduled to take effect on 1 April, the same date as the administration's directive.

'And I Was Beginning to Feel Sorry for Mr. Dulles!'
By permission of *The Washington Star*

By mid-February, Walsh and other leaders of the NGA decided that a public appeal against Bill 1017 was necessary if the Guard expected to retain its present program. Fearing that the Defense Department's directive, coupled with the passage of the proposed legislation, would destroy the incentives for enlisting, Walsh mounted a campaign to preserve the Guard's existing program.[23] On 18 February, he and several state National Guard officers testified before a subcommittee of the House Armed Services Committee against the proposed changes. Claiming that the six-month directive would be "the kiss of death" for the Guard, Walsh argued that the service would lose 50,000 enlistees annually if the Pentagon's wishes were followed. He maintained that the National Guard represented a guarantee against potential abuses of the professional military. The six-month program, Walsh stated, only signified the Army's intention to impose its own ill-conceived plan on the Guard. As an alternative, Walsh proposed that Congress require only eleven weeks of combat training for enlistees.[24]

After Walsh's testimony, several other National Guard commanders presented their views to the subcommittee. But the remarks of officers John W. Guerard, Roy Green, Melvin Maas, and Julius Klein proved to be the highlight of the hearings when these men broke with Walsh and supported both the administration and Senate proposals. Green and Guerard, both Californians, believed that the Guard's training procedures were inadequate. Green stated that he supported the Army's six-month training program, having seen many men die in his regiment during World War II in the fighting on Okinawa because they lacked sufficient training. Furthermore, he pointed out that the California National Guard had recently instituted the Army's plan and had not suffered any decline in enlistment. Guerard seconded Green's testimony, saying, "The day is gone when any lunkhead could have a rifle shoved in his hand and be ready to follow somebody with a saber who yelled charge."[25] On 20 February, Maas and Klein testified in Congress. Maas, a former congressman from Minnesota and major general in the Marine Corps, testified that the exemption of National Guard recruits from basic training exerted a negative effect on the entire reserve program. "Unless they receive more training," Maas stated, "National Guardsmen run the risk of being called draft-dodgers."[26] Klein, a guardsman from Illinois, also supported the idea of additional training but expressed his preference for the Senate proposal over that of the administration.

Thus the National Guard presented a divided front in its testimony. Walsh must have felt betrayed by the refusal of the other officers to support him. Furthermore, he received virtually no support from the press; even newspapers in his home state of Minnesota refused to support his position on the issue. A resident of Minneapolis, Walsh watched in dismay as the city's leading newspapers, the *Star* and *Tribune,* editorialized against the Guard's training program throughout February.[27] National publications had also swung around in support of Wilson by late February. Hanson Baldwin wrote in the *New York Times* on 23 February, "The Guard is not ready today and will not be ready tomorrow under existing conditions." Baldwin argued that Wilson's directive needed to be considered from the standpoint of the entire reserve program. "The Army's reforms," the columnist said, "are not intended to destroy the Guard, but to improve its readiness, and to require the same standards so claims of unfairness cannot be raised."

Wilson used the last week of February to strengthen his political position on the National Guard issue. On 22 February, he delivered an address to the Twenty-eighth Reconnaissance Corps of the Pennsylvania National Guard in Philadelphia. He stressed that while the National Guard had achieved its proper numerical strength, it had not attained the requisite degree of combat readiness. The proposed training program for new recruits had the support of the president, the Department of Defense, the Congress and a good number of state Guard commanders; the new directive would visibly strengthen the service.[28]

Wilson also instructed the civilian and military leadership of the Defense Department to appear before Congress and support the training proposal. On 23 February, Secretary of the Army Wilbur Brucker, Stephen Jackson, the assistant secretary of defense for manpower, and General Taylor testified before the House Armed Services Committee. Each man repeated Wilson's earlier assertion that the Pentagon's reforms were designed to improve the National Guard's training procedures. Brucker, who succeeded Stevens as Army secretary in 1955, also repeated Wilson's statement that 80 percent of the National Guard units were composed of men with no combat experience or training. Congress did not need to fear that the Guard's adoption of stricter training requirements would impair enlistment. In fact, enlistments in the Army Reserve had actually increased since the Army adopted the new plan in 1955.[29]

Congress's final decision on the matter involved a compromise between the Defense Department and the National Guard. Agreeing with the principle that new enlistees needed basic training, Congress nevertheless allowed the Guard nine months to implement the program. Wilson accepted Congress's advice on the matter and postponed the Pentagon's directive accordingly.[30]

The secretary's performance on the National Guard issue typified the type of determination he had shown throughout his career at the Pentagon. After making a serious and seemingly irreparable error in referring to the Guard's enlistment program as a "sort of scandal," he wisely admitted his mistake. Then, after clarifying the nature of his remarks, he proceeded to work for the necessary objective. The abrupt turnabout in public opinion, from outright condemnation of Wilson to vocal support for him, was due to the secretary's candor and the widespread recognition of the special training and enlistment privileges afforded to the National Guard in the past. Mrs. Wilson's spunky defense of her husband probably also helped the secretary.

By the end of February, little doubt remained that Wilson had chosen the correct policy regarding the National Guard, at least according to popular opinion. On 24 February, the *New York Herald-Tribune* published the results of a recent Gallup poll dealing with the controversy. By a 41 to 38 percent margin, those polled felt that the National Guard had been used as a haven for men wishing to avoid active service during the Korean War. More important, 65 percent of those questioned believed that recruits should receive the six months' training, as opposed to only 21 percent who considered the present procedures acceptable.[31]

Wilson apparently viewed the outcome of the controversy with some satisfaction. He later wrote to Carl Kindl, a longtime friend, thanking him for his expressions of support, and also discussing his impressions of the entire affair.

I appreciate your cartoon from the *Toronto Daily Star*—in fact my position with relation to the National Guard caused quite a deluge of cartoons all over the country. It looked for awhile that I might be in a little trouble, but actually it [the "draft-dodging" remark] got the real issues out on the table, and satisfactory results have been achieved.[32]

Wilson had perhaps unknowingly described the course of his career at the Pentagon. Certainly he was involved "in a little trouble" throughout his tenure at the Defense Department. Yet it can also be truthfully said that the secretary brought the real issues on national defense policy to the public's attention.

9

"Efficiency Experts Have Never Been Popular":
Wilson's Administration of the Defense Department

CHARLES E. Wilson wanted to devise a sound management structure for the Department of Defense. Less concerned than
his predecessors with strategic matters, he followed President Eisenhower's wishes in concentrating on improving the efficiency of the
department and exerting discipline on its spending. Wilson clearly
understood the president's wishes, once informing a Pentagon observer that he planned to "leave the military stuff up to the military,
the production up to us" (the Office of the Secretary of Defense).[1]
Although he underestimated the amount of time that he would later
spend on strategic matters as opposed to simply administrative ones,
his ability to bring order to the Pentagon's sprawling apparatus impressed many defense officials, both civilian and military. One of
Wilson's associates later remarked that in "the area of procurement,
[Wilson] had forgotten more than most guys knew."[2] Working closely
with Wilfred J. McNeil, the Pentagon comptroller, he used the budget
to determine the direction of defense policy. Such a procedure reflected a practical method of achieving greater civilian control over
the military, another of Eisenhower's national defense objectives.[3]

Wilson also followed some of Forrestal's practices in attempting to
manage the Defense Department. Like Forrestal, Wilson believed in
the importance of selecting skilled personnel to carry out defense
policy. To the extent possible, Wilson chose his civilian assistants on
the basis of merit and experience rather than appointing political or
personal favorites. McNeil, H. Struve Hensel, the department's first
general counsel and later an assistant secretary of defense for interna-

tional security affairs, and Charles Thomas, assistant secretary for supply and logistics, were men who performed well under Forrestal and continued to serve in the Wilson Pentagon. The exception to that rule may have been Roger M. Kyes, a former vice-president at General Motors whom Wilson persuaded to serve with him in Washington for a short time. Kyes was hardly a crony, however. A graduate of the Harvard School of Business and an exceptionally tough-minded executive who made the General Motors truck operation profitable, Kyes worked with McNeil on budgetary matters during his stay at the Pentagon.[4] Wilson also practiced Forrestal's philosophy of maintaining policy controls at the level of the secretary of defense while providing latitude to the various civilian and military personnel charged with implementing that policy. Unlike Louis Johnson, and like Forrestal, Wilson preferred to work through recognized staff channels, relying on the service secretaries, undersecretaries, and assistant secretaries of defense for administrative work. In military matters, Wilson conferred often with the JCS and considered Admiral Radford his principal military adviser.

Eisenhower's concept of the proper role for the secretary of defense and the "practical wisdom" which he acquired through conferences with his predecessors influenced Wilson's perception of the office, but he also possessed some definite ideas of his own about how to improve the Defense Department's administrative effectiveness. While at General Motors, Wilson had had occasion to observe the Pentagon's operation, especially after the outbreak of the Korean War, when the Truman administration submitted orders for emergency war material. Wilson believed strongly in the utility of Alfred P. Sloan's organizational principles and intended to put his philosophy into practice at the Pentagon, believing that such principles would improve the way in which defense production was handled during the war. The introduction of the General Motors organizational and administrative practices at the Defense Department shocked many Washington observers. Nevertheless, Wilson's decision to employ corporate managerial procedures and objectives was not made in haste, but rather after he had considered it for some time.

The major criticism directed against Wilson's corporate approach to the administration of the national defense program was that the

Pentagon was not a business; there was no means to compare, for example, the profitability of a business and the effectiveness of a government agency.[5] It should be remembered, however, that steps to remodel the defense establishment along business lines to achieve greater efficiency had already been taken with the legislation enacted during the Truman administration. Wilson's major doubt about the effectiveness of this legislation was his belief that it had centralized the national defense bureaucracy without providing an organization which would promote the coordination of responsibilities which it sought.[6] Wilson believed that Sloan's philosophy of coordinated policy and decentralized administration, if applied to the defense establishment, could result in improved management which provided a stronger defense program at an economical cost. While serving as secretary of defense, Wilson corresponded with Sloan concerning his use of the General Motors organizational principles at the Defense Department.[7] Wilson proposed to establish a business management system which would assist in developing immediate and long-range goals while also modernizing the military establishment.

Wilson's administrative plan involved two principles: policy control, achieved primarily through his use of the budget, and decentralized administration, achieved through a new management structure. Central to both principles was the defense reorganization of 1953 as recommended by Reorganization Plan 6 of the Rockefeller Committee. Under this plan, the secretary of defense received six additional assistant secretaries, who were responsible for "functional areas"— research and development, supply and logistics, properties and installations, legislative and public affairs, and the like.[8] Wilson's use of the assistant secretaries was pivotal to his overall management of the Pentagon. They took over the functions of the abolished boards and agencies but also assisted Wilson in maintaining policy control (Wilson's term was "the auditing of activities") over the military operation. According to Wilson's reorganization, the assistant secretaries corresponded to corporate vice-presidents who monitored Pentagon activities and kept the secretary (or corporation "president") informed on the department's progress. Wilson even referred to them as "my vice-presidents" and provided them with increasing supervisory responsibilities in their designated areas. Wilson's inauguration of "Operation Clean Sweep" in 1953, under the direction of Assistant Secretaries Charles Thomas and Franklin Floete, was an example of his inclination to strengthen his office's control over military activities. Operation Clean Sweep was a massive, worldwide inventory of the Defense Department's assets and supplies which lasted for over a year. Thomas and Floete presided over the sale of several hundred millions of dollars worth of surplus supplies and outmoded equipment. Upon completion of the operation, Wilson authorized the creation of a single supply and procurement catalogue for the armed services. The total saving to the Defense Department was estimated at $1 billion.[9]

The use of the assistant secretaries and Wilson's own managerial preferences helped him to establish a better business management system at the Pentagon. In attempting to stabilize costs and initiate long-term defense planning, the secretary employed the principle of decentralized administration. The Rockefeller Committee had recommended a further decentralization of defense administration, and Wilson understood the concept as well as any executive. Under Sloan, Wilson had supervised a highly decentralized General Motors operation, and he recognized that the leader of any large organization must delegate responsibility to subordinates within the confines of an accepted policy if the organization is to be successful. Wilson once attributed his success at General Motors to the fact that he "didn't have to eat the elephant all by myself." The test of good leadership, he believed, was the placement of responsibility upon those in position to act within the framework of certain broad policies.[10] The wise delegation of both responsibility and authority was imperative to the success of this administrative scheme.

Wilson adapted the recommendations of the Rockefeller Committee to establish a staff-and-line organization at the department, and the structure of the Office of the Secretary of Defense (OSD) assumed much importance. In business parlance, the OSD resembled a holding company for three subsidiaries, the Army, Navy, and Air Force. The secretary of defense's responsibility lay in policy control, and the individual service secretaries became responsible for management, or "running" the various "companies."[11] Military leaders served as advisers to both the armed service secretaries and the secretary of defense.

Each armed service had its own sphere of action, made decisions regarding its leadership, and mapped its own operations. Shortly after leaving office in 1957, Wilson explained the similarity between the defense organization and that of his previous corporate employer.

> We really had General Motors organized on a staff-and-line basis, very similar to the way the Department of Defense is now organized. We had operating divisions which would correspond to the Army, Navy, and Air Force. [The main responsibilities] were to clarify your policy and simplify the administration, fix responsibilities and delegate authority, [and make] the boss responsible in the final results of every activity.[12]

Decentralization also meant that Wilson intended to allow a degree of competition between the armed services for the development and acquisition of new weapons systems, especially in the ballistic missiles area, where the Army and Air Force carried on a vigorous contest for funds over several years. The competition between the services was intended to be reserved for the research and testing stages of development, however. Wilson seriously frowned on duplication once the system reached the production and procurement stage. Although he later revised his opinions somewhat on the matter of interservice competition, Wilson initially believed that competitive interplay between the services would "instill a sense of responsibility in each command."[13] Competition between the services for military weapons systems, however, seemed to some observers a strange way to administer a national defense program. Even so, Eisenhower also believed that such a procedure stood the best chance of arriving at workable programs. Although interservice competition remained built into the defense operation, Wilson's administrative structure emphasizing policy control, and his use of the budget as a policing vehicle, made it possible for him to decide the limits of existing policies. As Comptroller McNeil once stated, money was the source of the program's work; "If you turn on the faucet and shut it off, things will happen."[14] The trick, of course, was to know when to open and close the faucet.

If Wilson brought much of the General Motors management philosophy with him to Washington, so also did he bring his own personal brand of leadership. He had little liking for written reports, memoranda, and the other staples of bureaucracy. If problems

"Leave Something for Me, Charlie"

From *Herblock's Special for Today* (Simon & Schuster, 1958)

existed or decisions needed to be made, he preferred to deal with the personnel most directly involved on a specific matter. He gathered the information for defense decision making from discussions with Eisenhower, members of the National Security Council, cabinet members, the Joint Chiefs, and his civilian assistants. Depending on the severity of the issue, Wilson's conferring process could last weeks or months. As one observer noted, the secretary did not make "lightning decisions. He can make a fast decision [when necessary] but time permitting, he explores a problem with an exhausting and almost exasperating thoroughness." Such behavior was a carryover from his days in Detroit, where Wilson's seemingly endless conferences were labeled "C. E.'s World Tours" by fatigued automobile executives.[15]

Those who endured "C. E.'s World Tours" at the Defense Department either applauded or condemned Wilson's administrative style. It was clear that some military officers and an occasional civilian staffer felt impatient with the secretary's style of leadership. Maxwell Taylor and Matthew Ridgway, for example, objected to Wilson's loquaciousness and believed that it was time-consuming and ineffective. Some of Wilson's other associates believed that his lengthy conferences served to bring out many different viewpoints on complex issues and were helpful in making decisions which represented the thinking of many officials. Other individuals believed that the conferences satisfied Wilson's desire to get "all the facts" and provide the opportunity for those who opposed his thinking to state their positions. Wilson strongly believed that individuals with key defense responsibilities should have the opportunity honestly to state their positions before him. Time-consuming it may have been, but this practice allowed Wilson to get a wide range of opinions on defense matters and keep from being insulated. This openness also made him a fairly well-respected executive. Thomas Gates, one of Wilson's associates and later himself a secretary of defense, once remarked that Wilson "ran the Department of Defense by the human, as opposed to the machine method."[16]

Wilson also traveled extensively in his official capacity to visit military installations and defense plants. Before taking office in 1953, Wilson had used the occasion of his trip to Korea with Eisenhower as a way of meeting the three- and four-star officers stationed in the Far East. The secretary participated actively in the various Armed Forces

Wilson frequently toured defense production facilities, sometimes recommending specific improvements in plant procedures.

By permission of the Wilson Archives

Wilson on 17 May 1954, reviewing a South Korean honor guard with U.S. military leaders. Left to right: Wilson; Undersecretary of the Navy Thomas S. Gates; General John E. Hull; General Maxwell D. Taylor.

By permission of the Wilson Archives

Day ceremonies and, acting on suggestions by his associates, held an annual service secretaries conference at Quantico, Virginia, involving the Pentagon's civilian and military leadership. These conferences permitted Wilson to bring together the Pentagon's key civilian and military officials for a comprehensive review of defense issues. In many respects, Wilson patterned them after those which General Motors regularly scheduled for its executives.[17]

Wilson had always been interested in solving organizatonal problems, and, as defense secretary, intended to improve the Pentagon's production and procurement activities. He had witnessed the massive production problems at General Motors when the Korean War erupted and the Truman administration had to meet the crisis with an emergency mobilization effort. Before becoming secretary, Wilson believed that the nation lacked an adequate industrial base to handle the tremendously costly job of equipping the country for war at a timely speed. He thought that Congress should enact legislation providing for the construction of dual purpose plants, containing storage space for either civilian or defense equipment. Wilson possessed blueprints of these proposed plants and hoped to get some congressional action on his idea while he remained in office, claiming that such legislation was necessary as part of an overall national defense program.[18]

Such legislation was not forthcoming when the Korean War ended, and a "business as usual" approach to peacetime defense production ensued. The continuing demand for preparedness, however, caused a number of production bottlenecks when the Pentagon placed sizable orders with the nation's industries. One such difficulty occurred during 1954 and involved Republic Aviation, which was running behind in its production of the F-84F aircraft. Wilson visited Republic's plant in Farmingdale, Long Island, and discovered that Air Force planners had rushed their production of the plane before perfecting the design. Along with Fred Seaton, assistant secretary of defense for legislative affairs, Wilson spent one day touring the plant and was briefed on the problems which Republic faced. He discussed the problems with Republic's managers and suggested a method of internal factory organization which might be better suited to increased production. One observer claimed that Wilson's recommendations constituted the "most marvelous exhibition of plant analysis he had ever seen."[19]

The organizational structure which Wilson devised and his own administrative style served him acceptably in dealing with the two major problem areas which he encountered during his tenure: coordinating the administration's economic and budgetary policy with the wishes of the military leadership and selling these policies to Congress. He had a critical role, for the secretary of defense had to be an individual of sufficient ability to maintain the confidence of the military and of congressmen and senators. Keeping the military leaders disciplined to the administration's economic policy proved to be Wilson's most difficult task. Eisenhower served notice early that he expected the Joint Chiefs to consider scientific, industrial, and economic factors in their planning and refrain from offering simply military advice based on their respective parochial viewpoints. In Wilson's words, the Joint Chiefs were to be "members of the team, not spokesmen for it."[20]

As Wilson's experience at the Defense Department demonstrated, some military leaders had difficulty adapting their thinking to the Eisenhower-Wilson-Humphrey approach to defense policy. Eisenhower believed in maintaining a ceiling on defense spending during a given fiscal year, although he preferred to refer to it as a "target" or "guideline." This policy served to make the JCS and the various armed services especially concerned about the internal distribution of defense appropriations, but, by 1957, both Eisenhower and Wilson believed that the military had accommodated itself to the concept of an overall ceiling on military spending. Wilson of course was comfortable with this approach; the General Motors procedure also emphasized "tight control of money" at the executive level.[21] For the Joint Chiefs, reaching a consensus on strategic policy was more a response to the instructions of Eisenhower, Wilson, and Radford than a decision made according to military preferences.

For his part, Wilson left the Pentagon in 1957 convinced that the organizational reforms and administrative procedures which he instituted brought about a better measure of responsibility in the civilian-military budgetary process. He stated, "Even with the military, there is a final recognition that economic and political strength are a necessary part of military strength. They understand that we can't have a strong military force and not have a strong economy to back it up."[22]

Budget ceilings and civilian reviews of military activity by Wilson's assistants, however, hardly made the secretary a favorite among some influential military leaders. General James Gavin claimed that the secretary "tended to deal with his Chiefs of Staff as though they were recalcitrant union bosses," and argued that Wilson lacked the knowledge of military affairs necessary to perform effectively at the Pentagon. Such criticism had little impact on Wilson's professional thinking, although he was personally concerned about it, and once revealed his attitude at a Pentagon news conference. Asked if he "found a great deal of inertia in the military establishment," he replied: "Well, of course, they would like to run their own particular service and not ever have anybody check up on it. That is just human nature. I know the efficiency experts have never been popular, so I don't worry about that."[23]

Wilson's stand on budgetary restraint was not the most conservative position in the administration, however. George Humphrey and Eisenhower's budget directors, Joseph Dodge and Percival Brundage, consistently urged Wilson to make reductions which the secretary felt were inappropriate. In such instances, Eisenhower sometimes needed to settle the matter, usually by supporting Wilson's estimates, as he did in 1953, 1955, and 1957.[24]

Two other factors contributed to Wilson's problems in keeping the defense budget within the confines of administration policy. One was the New Look's concentration on nuclear weapons and advanced missile systems. As Wilson's term in office continued, the bills for such complex innovations as the Titan, Atlas, Thor, and Jupiter missile systems started to come due and at a higher cost than the original estimates. The so-called cost overrun became reality, and by 1957 some of Eisenhower's White House staffers believed that Wilson was losing hold on the Pentagon's fiscal machinery. Wilson felt the pressure as well, remarking at one time that he felt "like a frog trying to jump out of a well" in trying to stabilize defense costs.[25]

Although defense costs were on the rise by 1957, it was an exaggeration to suggest that Wilson had lost control of the programming. Inflation had pushed up the costs of major weapons by 18 percent since 1954; there was also a 15 percent increase in military personnel costs and an 11 percent jump in equipment maintenance expenditures during the same period. In late 1956 and early 1957, Wilson had labored mightily to bring down defense expenditures "billion by painful billion" to the $38 billion target established by Eisenhower. In recounting Wilson's efforts at economizing, Budget Director Brundage remarked that the secretary "really wrestled with this budget. You could actually see him sweat."[26] As time went on, Wilson found himself sandwiched between Treasury Department officials who continued to hope, somewhat unrealistically, for a reduction in defense spending below the $35 billion mark, and the reality of the costs for high technology hardware. By 1957, Wilson's functional improvements had wrung out about all that could be expected in nonprogrammatic savings. Any future reductions would have involved sizable changes in the research and development or strategic areas. Wilson was not inclined to favor such cutbacks.

In addition to the increased costs of the Pentagon's procurement programs, the changing congressional attitude on military spending occasionally caused complications for Wilson. For example, Congress authorized a $900 million supplement to the defense budget in 1956. In the following year, however, Congress wanted to reduce the budget which Wilson presented. "I didn't think the Russians were 10 feet tall last year but I don't think they're only 5 feet tall this year," the secretary told the Senate Appropriations Committee. "We simply can't have these emotional swings back and forth and expect to do a decent job for the country."[27] Indeed, Eisenhower once described exactly this situation in a White House meeting, when he warned Wilson and his civilian assistants about the tendency of Congress to change its mind on defense spending from year to year. "Put every person on the spot to justify every nickel," the president told Wilson in 1956. "Next year the demagogues will all be gone and everybody will be looking to save money."[28]

The administration and management of the Defense Department was a highly complex task, and Wilson came to realize that it involved not only the application of sound organizational principles but also effective relations with Congress, the military, and the Treasury Department and continual attention to fiscal details. By 1957, the results of Wilson's administrative performance at the Pentagon were apparent, however. In strictly administrative terms, he had followed the recommendations of the Rockefeller Committee in establishing a decentralized, staff-and-line management structure. More important, however, the new structure enabled him to establish a measure of policy control based on the use of the Pentagon's budget which strengthened the civilian supervision of the military's activities. His own knowledge of management techniques and efficiency measures contributed to saving over $1 billion during his first two years in office. In directing the Pentagon's vast procurement and development programs, Wilson walked a tightrope between military demands for preparedness and the White House and Treasury's demand for economy. The occasional tendency of Congress to press for either more or less military spending was a periodic irritant. By late 1957, as Wilson prepared to leave the Defense Department, it was fair to ask whether his business-oriented leadership had served the nation better than the various administrative styles of his predecessors.

An objective assessment of Wilson's managerial performance requires a mixed evaluation. On the positive side, Wilson's efficiency measures had resulted in saving a vast amount of money. Certainly his introduction of a General Motors style of management structure helped to bring more civilian control over the military and it served as a model for future defense secretaries. In strategic matters, the position of American armed might improved as compared with that of the Soviet Union. The new weapons systems developed during the Wilson years, especially the ICBM and IRBM missiles, created a technological pressure which the Russians were hard pressed to match.[29]

Did Wilson succeed in his goal of establishing a business management system which provided for long-term stability in defense programming? He did win Eisenhower's approval to submit a three-year defense program beginning with fiscal year 1958. But even Wilson's cost-conscious Pentagon administration failed to reduce defense spending to the $35 billion mark that many in the administration desired. As his term of office continued, he even resisted the pressure from some of Eisenhower's budgeteers to reduce defense spending below the level submitted in the Pentagon's annual request to Congress. By 1957, Wilson clearly had become involved in the dilemma of determining how much defense the nation needed to buy in order to conduct a successful foreign policy, protect the nation, and yet permit the economy to function relatively unhampered. More than any other single political leader of the 1950s (with President Eisenhower as the exception), Wilson came to realize that the arms competition between the United States and the Soviet Union required larger defense outlays than America had ever provided for its military establishment in peacetime.[30]

10
Wilson in Perspective

C HARLES E. Wilson officially resigned as secretary of defense on 8 October 1957. He held a farewell press conference on 2 October to discuss the current status of the Defense Department and reflect on the events of the previous four-and-a-half years. Wilson invited his wife to attend the briefing with him, and when the couple entered the Pentagon's conference room, the assembled reporters greeted them with a standing ovation. The press conference proceeded lightheartedly. Wilson explained, for what must have seemed the thousandth time, the real intent behind his remark that "what was good for our country was good for General Motors and vice versa." One reporter asked if the nation had ever "been to the brink of war" during Wilson's tenure at the Pentagon. To the considerable amusement of the press, the secretary replied, "You'd better ask the Secretary of State about that."[1]

Throughout the conference, Wilson emphasized that the Defense Department faced some serious and complex problems in the future. He was, however, reasonably satisfied with the progress which the military establishment had made while he was secretary of defense. Although he refused to list his accomplishments during the meeting, Wilson could have mentioned a number of improvements which he introduced. He had assumed his responsibilities at the Defense Department at a crucial time in the midst of the Korean War. After helping to manage that war effort, he had tried to bring systematic management to the defense operation once the hostilities ended. By establishing an organizational structure which improved the effectiveness of the Pentagon's work, he succeeded in implementing some administrative changes which his predecessors had recommended but had been unable to carry out. Fully mindful of the importance of recent technological developments to the military establishment, Wilson began a modernization of the armed forces, presiding over the Eisenhower administration's decisions to emphasize nuclear weapons technology instead of conventional war capability. The massive changes which occurred in the research and development of these weapons systems strengthened the nation's military might. In defending the administration's approach to defense policy, one of Wilson's associates later remarked that the secretary sought "to reduce manpower costs and not put all the eggs in the wrong basket."[2]

Wilson's major contribution to the secretary's office was his stable leadership. None of his predecessors had lasted more than eighteen months in office, and Wilson himself became discouraged at the high rate of turnover among both civilian and millitary personnel. He made a commitment to Eisenhower, however, that he would serve at least one presidential term, provided he retained the president's confidence; he believed that any long-term progress at the Defense Department would be impossible if there were frequent changes of secretary. He also encouraged his associates to remain in office. Moreover, Wilson's tenure as defense secretary came at a time when a clear-cut distinction needed to be made between the military and its civilian leadership. By holding the office almost five years, Wilson ensured that important national security policy decisions made at the presidential level were not ignored.[3] He succeeded in carrying out Eisenhower's proposed $5 billion reduction in defense costs after the Korean War, for instance, and he kept those costs fairly stable over the next four years.

Like any public official, however, Wilson encountered difficulties in the political arena. His relations with Congress, and particularly with the Senate, were never cordial. Yet, given the nature of the political issues involving national defense, it is doubtful that any active secretary of defense could win the lasting respect or admiration of the entire Congress. Wilson occasionally experienced problems with the military, too. But with Eisenhower's assistance, he managed to restrain the military within the confines of administration policy.[4]

Finally, what can be said about Wilson's controversial career as secretary of defense? Was his administrative performance sufficient to bring order to a vast, sometimes chaotic, bureaucracy? Were the controversial decisions which he made appropriate to the realities of a sound defense in the nuclear age?

There were some who would answer no to these questions. General Gavin, for instance, once quoted a colleague as saying that Wilson "was the most uninformed man, and the most determined to remain so, that has ever been Secretary."[5] Certainly, Senators Russell, Johnson, Kefauver, and others shared the military's doubt about Wilson's ability. In making their criticisms, however, Wilson's political and military detractors overlooked the fact that the secretary was in Washington to implement a defense policy, not to devise one. Wilson understood well where his responsibilities lay. Fearful of runaway defense spending, Eisenhower had instructed him to be an economizer. By the end of his tenure, Wilson had experienced at first hand the momentum toward institutionalizing the nation's military requirements in the general economy. A harbinger of Eisenhower's warning in his 1961 farewell address against the emergence of a "military-industrial complex," Wilson told the Senate Subcommittee on Defense Appropriations in 1957: "One of the serious things about this defense business is that so many Americans are getting a vested interest in it; properties, business, jobs, employment, votes, opportunities for promotion and advancement, bigger salaries for scientists and all that. It is a troublesome business."[6] One warning was given by a cabinet member who was publicly viewed as the military's advocate in the government, and the other by a president whose entire adult career had been spent in the armed services. One would not normally expect criticism of the military from individuals with those responsibilities and background.

If Wilson was primarily a manager, rather than a planner, then Gavin's criticism of him missed the point. When naming him secretary of defense, Eisenhower spoke of Wilson's administrative experience. In criticizing New Look strategy, Gavin was essentially criticizing Eisenhower's military judgment, as it was the president who established the outline of the administration's defense policy. Gavin, of course, had every right to criticize the president; one should not believe, however, that his views were necessarily superior to those of

Eisenhower. As for Wilson's skill as an administrator, one of his associates remarked that the secretary's "way takes patience, but for results and long-range policies, I've never seen anybody up to [him]."[7] Given the reality of Eisenhower as the planner and Wilson as the manager, it was necessary for the secretary of defense sometimes to act as an adversary to military leaders who wanted larger appropriation and manpower levels. For a secretary of defense to be an adversary of the military may be unusual (Gavin certainly did not like it), but Wilson often occupied that controversial position.

And what of strategy? Was Wilson's inexperience in military affairs and strategic planning a liability? One point does emerge: during the 1950s, the secretary never developed the fascination with guerilla warfare, counterinsurgency tactics, and the "Flexible Response" doctrine which became so popular with the Army staff and the liberal anti-Communist element of Congress. The unilateralist tendencies involved in such approaches to military programming bothered Wilson mightily. For example, when the situation in Indochina was reaching a serious crisis in May 1954, Wilson told a news conference that the United States could not assume responsibility for intervening in local conflicts.

> Our basic responsibility is to protect our nation and the nations of the free world. We can't take the sole responsibility of trying to please the whole world. As strong and powerful as our nation is, we can't do that alone.
> Also, even if we tried it, we'd be misunderstood in the effort, and you know, even good policemen aren't popular very long. We'd soon lose all our friends if we approached the world from that angle.[8]

It seemed to Wilson that the theories of his critics in the military, supported in Congress by Russell, Symington, Johnson, Jackson, Humphrey, and Kennedy, went against the grain of the collective security consensus which emerged during the early Cold War. Eisenhower and Truman (but to a lesser extent) believed in the importance of alliances and in allies bearing the responsibility for local defense. Wilson's detractors seemed to be arguing that such an approach would not work. Because of Eisenhower's opposition to a worldwide American military presence, "Flexible Response" lived on short rations during the 1950s. But in the 1960s, the counterinsurgency, limited war capability concept won widespread acceptance and even popular support, only to be tested in the jungles of South-east Asia. Importantly, Wilson's opposition to "Flexible Response" did not arise from any sophisticated military planning rationale, but rather from his belief that the doctrine violated some fundamental defense objectives of the administration.

Even though Wilson was often the center of controversy, he was fortunate to have Eisenhower's support throughout his tenure. His-torically, presidents have chosen their secretaries of defense from four different areas. Several, including Forrestal, Lovett, Gates, and Clark Clifford, have come from the world of investment banking and corporate law. George C. Marshall possessed extensive military and bureaucratic experience; Louis Johnson, Melvin Laird, and Donald Rumsfeld held previous political offices. Wilson, Neil McElroy, and Robert McNamara were industrialists. James Schlesinger and Harold Brown were associated with universities and public policy research institutions. Eisenhower chose Wilson to be secretary of defense in an administrative capacity; the president intended to concern himself with the larger military issues. The secretary of defense assumed even greater managerial responsibility for his department when Eisenhower suffered a heart attack in 1955. Wilson did not have to worry about the intricacies of military planning because he knew that the general in the White House was fully capable in that area. It is open to speculation, however, whether an industrialist-manager makes an effective defense secretary if the president he serves lacks a wide range of military understanding. In the absence of such a presi-dent, the secretary of defense needs to be thoroughly grounded in military doctrines in order to keep from being swayed by partisan service representatives.

Wilson was one of Eisenhower's most important cabinet members, a secretary of defense who provided the kind of leadership that the president outlined for the position when he took office in 1953. The secretary was more than the humorous man who once remarked, "A little bit of aggression is like a little bit of pregnancy," or who, in analyzing the bureaucratic competition between the Army and the Air Force over a new weapons system, said that he could not "understand it, unless the Army and Air Force plan on fighting each other."[9] With Eisenhower's assistance, Wilson proved to be a durable, pragmatic, and competent executive.

Notes

CHAPTER ONE

1. Accounts of the Eisenhower administration may be separated into those written by journalists during the 1950s and early 1960s and those written by historians during the 1970s. Works which discuss Wilson's role in the administration include: Robert J. Donovan, *Eisenhower*, pp. 9–10; Marquis Childs, *Eisenhower*, pp. 170–71; Emmett John Hughes, *The Ordeal of Power*, pp. 75–76; Herbert S. Parmet, *Eisenhower and the American Crusades*, pp. 170–71, 188–89; Townsend Hoopes, *The Devil and John Foster Dulles*, pp. 137–40; Charles C. Alexander, *Holding the Line*, pp. 31–32; and Douglas Kinnard, *President Eisenhower and Strategy Management*, pp. 20, 21, 24, 25, 29. Memoirs written by members of the administration include: Sherman Adams, *Firsthand Report;* Ezra Taft Benson, *Crossfire;* Arthur Larson, *Eisenhower;* Richard M. Nixon, *Six Crises;* and Lewis Strauss, *Men and Decisions.*

2. Childs, *Eisenhower*, pp. 170–72; Hughes, *Ordeal of Power*, p. 75; Emmett John Hughes, *The Living Presidency*, p. 153.

3. Donovan, *Eisenhower*, pp. 9–10; Parmet, *Eisenhower and the American Crusades*, pp. 170–71.

4. Parmet, *Eisenhower and the American Crusades*, p. 173; Childs, *Eisenhower*, p. 171; Charles E. Wilson Archives, Anderson College, Anderson, Indiana, MSS Box 42, General Correspondence, "A–F"; MSS Box 43, General Correspondence, "G–M". Hereafter cited as WA, MSS box, item, and page.

5. Betty Beale, "Two of a Kind Size Each Other Up," *Chicago Tribune*, 6 August 1955. Beale wrote a point-by-point comparison of Wilson and Truman based on telephone interviews with each man. Wilson stated that he had found Truman "courteous and fair" in his dealings with him during World War II while Wilson was coordinating the defense production effort at General Motors. For his part, Truman believed that Wilson was "a fine person and I like him personally." Truman hastened to add, however, that Wilson "doesn't belong to my political breed."

6. WA, MSS Box 62, Minutes of Press Conference, the Pentagon, 4 March 1954, p. 9.
7. Daniel J. Boorstin, *The Americans: The Democratic Experience* (New York: Random House, 1973), p. 593.
8. Stephen E. Ambrose and Walter LaFeber have both given excellent analyses of the Eisenhower administration's decision making on political-military affairs. Ambrose explained in *Rise to Globalism:* "The Republicans rattled the saber and always they filled the air with denunciations of the communists, but they also shut down the Korean War, cut corporate taxes and reduced the size of the Armed Forces" (p. 220). His argument that "the Republicans were more determined to balance the budget and enjoy the fruits of capitalism than they were to support a war machine" (p. 241) succinctly states the relationship between domestic economic considerations and foreign policy.

   LaFeber has argued that domestic considerations are often determining influences on foreign policy. In pp. 128–98 of *America, Russia, and the Cold War, 1945–1975,* he describes the constraints on foreign policy exerted by Eisenhower's conservative economic program. "At each Cabinet meeting in which Dulles defended the free world against communism, Secretary Humphrey defended the Treasury against the prodigals, especially those who wanted larger budgets for conventional military forces. Dulles acquiesced in those views" (p. 177).
9. Ambrose, *Rise to Globalism*, pp. 188–91. The best account of NSC-68 may be found in Paul Y. Hammond's "NSC-68" in Warner R. Schilling, Paul Y. Hammond, and Glenn H. Snyder, *Strategy, Politics, and Defense Budgets,* pp. 267–378. See also Samuel P. Huntington, *The Common Defense,* pp. 47–53; Edward Kolodziej, *The Uncommon Defense and Congress, 1945–1963,* pp. 124–40; and Kinnard, *President Eisenhower and Strategy Management,* pp. 6, 7, 8.
10. *New York Times,* 26 September 1952.
11. Quoted in Kinnard, *President Eisenhower and Strategy Management,* p. 113.
12. Charles E. Wilson, "More Defense for Every Dollar," p. 31.
13. Ambrose, *Rise to Globalism,* p. 228; WA, MSS Box 62, Minutes of Press Conference, the Pentagon, 4 May 1953, p. 13.
14. Wilson, "More Defense for Every Dollar," p. 31.
15. See, for example, WA, "Addresses by C. E. Wilson," 1954, Speech to American Society of Newspaper Editors, Washington, D.C., 13 April 1954, pp. 1–4. In this speech Wilson appraised the role of new military technology in defense programming.
16. Ambrose states this argument clearly. "Since Eisenhower could not lead the nation into a nuclear war, and since he didn't have the troops to fight a limited war, nor could he get them from his allies, the only alternative left was peace of some kind with the Russians" (*Rise to Globalism,* p. 241).
17. Truman also was actively involved in defense policy, first by submitting legislation to create the Department of Defense and then by making each of his four secretaries of defense dependent upon his wishes in strategic and budgetary matters.

18. James David Barber, *The Presidential Character,* p. 163; Dan Rather and Gary Paul Gates, *The Palace Guard,* p. 15. See also Adams, *Firsthand Report,* p. 99; Hoopes, *Devil and John Foster Dulles,* p. 140.
19. Adams, *Firsthand Report,* pp. 404–5; Hughes, *Ordeal of Power,* pp. 75–76.
20. WA, MSS Box 69, Minutes of Press Conference, 21 May 1956, pp. 1–4.

CHAPTER TWO

1. WA, "Addresses by C. E. Wilson," 1953, statement by Secretary-designate Charles E. Wilson to Senate Armed Services Committee, 15 January 1953, p. 1.
2. Walter Millis, ed., *The Forrestal Diaries,* p. 299. The entry concerns a letter from Forrestal to Robert Sherwood, 27 August 1947, in which he commented on the magnitude of his task at the Pentagon.
3. C. W. Borklund, *The Department of Defense,* pp. 40–46, gives a brief summary of the National Security Act of 1947. A number of other studies discuss the formation of the Defense Department in broader detail: Paul Y. Hammond, *Organizing for Defense;* Huntington, *Common Defense;* Kolodziej, *Uncommon Defense and Congress;* and Schilling, Hammond, and Snyder, *Strategy, Politics, and Defense Budgets.* For works on the Truman administration dealing with the defense issue, see Bert Cochran, *Harry S. Truman and the Crisis Presidency,* pp. 287–88; Richard Haynes, *The Awesome Power,* pp. 107–10; and Truman's own *Memoirs,* vol. 2, *Years of Trial and Hope,* pp. 49–50, 59–60, 104–5.
4. Millis, ed., *Forrestal Diaries,* pp. 291–96; Haynes, *Awesome Power,* p. 94. See also Walter Millis, Harvey C. Mansfield, and Harold Stein, *Arms and the State,* pp. 287–88.
5. Millis, ed., *Forrestal Diaries,* p. 492; Cochran, *Harry S. Truman and the Crisis Presidency,* pp. 287–88.
6. Huntington, *Common Defense,* pp. 278–81.
7. Borklund, *Department of Defense,* pp. 54–55; Haynes, *Awesome Power,* p. 113; Truman, *Years of Trial and Hope,* p. 53.
8. See Millis, Mansfield, and Stein, *Arms and the State,* pp. 138–258. See also C. W. Borklund, *Men of the Pentagon,* pp. 12–23, 39–137, for brief profiles of each defense secretary in the Truman administration; and Hammond, *Organizing for Defense,* pp. 232–87.
9. James M. Roherty, *Decisions of Robert S. McNamara,* pp. 17–30.
10. Millis, ed., *Forrestal Diaries,* pp. 389, 392–93, 395–96; Cochran, *Harry S. Truman and the Crisis Presidency,* pp. 287–88; Kolodziej, *Uncommon Defense,* pp. 74–77.
11. Richard Collier, *Bridge across the Sky.* See also Dean Acheson, *Present at the Creation,* pp. 269–73; Herbert Feis, *From Trust to Terror,* pp. 341–46; Millis, ed., *Forrestal Diaries,* pp. 479–91.
12. Haynes, *Awesome Power,* pp. 139–46; Margaret Truman, *Harry S. Truman,* pp. 407–8; Borklund, *Men of the Pentagon,* p. 59.
13. Millis, ed., *Forrestal Diaries,* pp. 459, 461–62, 450–91.

14. Borklund, *Men of the Pentagon*, p. 49; Haynes, *Awesome Power*, pp. 139–45; Millis, ed., *Forrestal Diaries*, pp. 359–61, 362–63, 405–6, 410–11.
15. Millis, ed., *Forrestal Diaries*, p. 497.
16. Margaret Truman, *Harry S. Truman*, pp. 407–8; Millis, ed., *Forrestal Diaries*, pp. 546–47; Borklund, *Men of the Pentagon*, p. 47; Millis, Mansfield, and Stein, *Arms and the State*, pp. 220–22.
17. Borklund, *Men of the Pentagon*, p. 68.
18. Haynes, *Awesome Power*, pp. 124–26; Kolodziej, *Uncommon Defense*, p. 108.
19. Borklund, *Men of the Pentagon*, pp. 74–79; Millis, Mansfield, and Stein, *Arms and the State*, pp. 239–42, 244–45.
20. Acheson, *Present at the Creation*, p. 373; Hammond, Schilling, and Snyder, *Strategy, Politics, and Defense Budgets*, pp. 295–98; Margaret Truman, *Harry S. Truman*, pp. 478–79; Huntington, *Common Defense*, pp. 49–53; David S. McLellan, *Dean Acheson*, pp. 203–5.
21. Acheson, *Present at the Creation*, pp. 423–24.
22. Ibid., p. 441. Johnson's irascibility was attributed to a brain malady which later proved fatal.
23. Haynes, *Awesome Power*, pp. 192–94; Millis, Mansfield, and Stein, *Arms and the State*, pp. 234–36, 279; Truman, *Harry S. Truman*, pp. 478–79; H. Truman, *Years of Trial and Hope*, p. 362.
24. Borklund, *Men of the Pentagon*, pp. 101–2; Millis, Mansfield, and Stein, *Arms and the State*, pp. 181–82; Acheson, *Present at the Creation*, p. 441.
25. Borklund, *Men of the Pentagon*, pp. 110, 112.
26. Roherty, *Decisions of Robert S. McNamara*, p. 34; Borklund, *Men of the Pentagon*, pp. 130–31.
27. Millis, Mansfield, and Stein, *Arms and the State*, pp. 352–53, 355, 379.
28. David Halberstam, *The Best and the Brightest*, pp. 9–10.
29. See Linfield Myers, *As I Remember the Wilson-Morrison Years*, edited by Larry G. Osnes (Anderson, Ind.: Anderson College Press, 1973), pp. 27–48, 49–76, for comments on Wilson's early business career. A good profile of Wilson's life may also be found in Beverly Smith, "Secretary Wilson's Year of Trial," *Saturday Evening Post*, May 1954. See also Borklund, *Men of the Pentagon*, pp. 139–40.
30. *U.S. News and World Report*, 30 December 1949, pp. 33–34.
31. Myers, *As I Remember the Wilson-Morrison Years*, pp. 30–31; Smith, "Secretary Wilson's Year of Trial," p. 114.
32. WA, MSS Box 50, Charles E. Wilson to Alfred P. Sloan, 17 January 1955, p. 3. This letter from Wilson to Sloan recounts Wilson's business career. At the time, Sloan was gathering material for his future book, *My Years with General Motors*, and had requested that Wilson and other key General Motors executives with whom he had worked while president and, later, chairman of the corporation provide written comments about their experiences in the automobile industry. Wilson's letter includes much biographical detail which helps to place his administrative and managerial philosophy in perspective. See also Smith, "Secretary Wilson's Year of Trial," pp. 18–19.

33. Borklund, *Men of the Pentagon,* pp. 15–16.
34. WA, MSS Box 50, Wilson to Sloan, 17 January 1955, pp. 15–16; see Peter F. Drucker, *The Unseen Revolution,* pp. 5–9, for an analysis of the profound effect which Wilson's pension scheme has had on the American economy.
35. William T. Serrin, *The Company and the Union,* pp. 20, 159–60, 177–78; *New York Times,* 27 September 1961.
36. Roherty, *Decisions of Robert S. McNamara,* pp. 17–18.
37. Peter F. Drucker, *Management,* pp. 137–47.

CHAPTER THREE

1. Hughes, *Ordeal of Power,* p. 76.
2. Senate Committee on Armed Services, *Department of Defense Nominations,* 1953, 83d. Cong., 1st sess., pp. 7–10, 34. Wilson requested that a letter to him from Alfred P. Sloan be placed into the record of the hearings. This letter, dated 15 January 1953, detailed Wilson's participation in the various compensation plans available to him as a result of his past service to the corporation.
3. *New Republic,* 15 December 1953, p. 15; see also Parmet, *Eisenhower and the American Crusades,* pp. 172–94. In addition to Wilson, Dulles, Brownell, and Humphrey, other cabinet members were Douglas McKay (Interior), Ezra Taft Benson (Agriculture), Arthur Summerfield (postmaster general), Sinclair Weeks (Commerce), and Martin Durkin (Labor). Eisenhower's concern that the administration's probusiness orientation might be a liability was evident when he warned the cabinet at one of its first meetings, "We have to be careful that this administration is truly interested in the little fellow, not just the banks and the corporations" (Hughes, *Ordeal of Power,* pp. 76–77).
4. WA, MSS Box 35, Correspondence with Dwight D. Eisenhower. Wilson's correspondence with Eisenhower in the years before the 1952 election indicates that he may have been interested in a post in a future Eisenhower administration. Wilson's speeches demonstrated that he may have been thinking not only of the Defense Department but also of the Commerce Department or the Bureau of the Budget.
5. Dwight D. Eisenhower, *Mandate for Change,* p. 86.
6. *Christian Science Monitor,* 21 November 1952; *Washington Post,* 23 November 1952.
7. James T. Patterson, *Mr. Republican,* p. 583. Taft may have been bitter over Wilson's open support of Eisenhower before the opening of the Republican national convention in 1952 and his efforts to convince Arthur Summerfield, the chairman of the Michigan delegation, to throw his support behind the general. See Carl Solberg, *Riding High,* p. 211.
8. For the legal complexities involved in Wilson's nomination, see Lyon, *Eisenhower,* p. 466; and Parmet, *Eisenhower and the American Crusades,* pp. 170–71. See C. Wright Mills, *The Power Elite,* pp. 168, 285, 355; and Richard M. Polenberg, *War and Society,* pp. 10–12, 75, 90–91, for accounts of the role of businessmen in national defense programs.

9. Borklund, *Men of the Pentagon,* pp. 79, 141–42.
10. Senate Committee on Armed Services, *Department of Defense Nominations,* 1953, pp. 14–15. See also Lyon, *Eisenhower,* pp. 505–6.
11. Senate Committee on Armed Services, *Department of Defense Nominations,* 1953, p. 30.
12. Ibid., pp. 25–26.
13. This was Wilson's most frequently quoted, or misquoted, remark during his tenure in Washington, D.C. The secretary always maintained that he placed country ahead of corporation. See WA, MSS Box 63, Minutes of Press Conference, 2 October 1957. Other writers have noted the discrepancy between Wilson's statement in the hearings and the one which has survived in public memory. William Manchester noted in *The Glory and the Dream* (Boston: Little, Brown, 1974), pp. 648–49, how Wilson's critics distorted his testimony. Even so, Manchester begins his discussion of the Eisenhower years with a chapter entitled "What Was Good for General Motors" (p. 643).
14. WA, MSS Box 50, Testimony regarding General Motors Postwar Program to Special Committee on Postwar Planning of the House of Representatives, 24 May 1953, p. 39. This document was reprinted by permission by General Motors Corporation and contains material excerpted from the congressional hearings of Wilson's testimony to the committee, popularly known as the Colmer Committee after its chairman, William Colmer.
15. WA, MSS Box 50, Testimony to Special Committee of the United States Senate to investigate the National Defense Program, 24 November 1943, p. 17. This document was reprinted by permission by General Motors Corporation from the Congressional hearings and contains material excerpted from Wilson's Senate testimony.
16. *Washington Evening Star,* 20 January 1953; *New York Post,* 23 January 1953.
17. In one particularly anxious moment of the hearings, when Wilson appeared unable to convince the committee that he had found a satisfactory way to avoid conflict of interest, he asked, "What do you men want me to do with my money?" See Senate Committee on Armed Services, *Department of Defense Nominations,* 1953, p. 114. For the committee's disapproval of Wilson's behavior, see Borklund, *Men of the Pentagon,* p. 141.
18. *Washington Post,* 20 January 1953; Eisenhower, *Mandate for Change,* p. 112.
19. Lyon, *Eisenhower,* p. 506.
20. Senate Committee on Armed Services, *Department of Defense Nominations,* 1953, pp. 107, 109.
21. Ibid., pp. 7, 14, 138–39. The Sloan-Wilson letter of 15 January 1953 adequately presents the extent of Wilson's participation in the bonus plan as well as the corporation's method of administering it. Sloan stated that the General Motors Bonus and Salary Committee, a group of individuals not in the employ of General Motors, responsible for administering the bonus and salary program, ruled that any "action or conduct by you while

serving as Secretary of Defense will not be regarded as inimical or in any way contrary to the best interests of General Motors Corporation."

22. Ibid., p. 140.
23. Ibid., pp. 144–45.
24. The *New York Times,* 27 January 1953, gives the details of Wilson's deliberations with the counsel for the General Motors Bonus and Salary Committee. The General Motors proxy statement of 22 May 1953 affirmed the completion of settling Wilson's finances.
25. *New York Times,* 27 January 1953.
26. Lyon, *Eisenhower,* pp. 506–7; WA, MSS Box 184, Memorandum for the Record, 22 January 1953. See also Parmet, *Eisenhower and the American Crusades,* p. 171.
27. For example, in "Few Hurt in Wilson Affair," *Washington Evening Star,* 28 January 1953, David Lawrence complimented Wilson for his "patience and determination" and lamented that the "net effect of this episode will be to discourage capable people from joining the government." For a critical view of Wilson's performance, see Arthur M. Schlesinger, Jr.'s column in the *New York Post,* 28 January 1953. Schlesinger claimed that the administration demonstrated "incredible stupidity" in its handling of Wilson's nomination. "The business community has always botched the job when it tried to govern the country," he wrote, saying that the Wilson episode provided "more evidence of the chronic incapacity of businessmen for government."
28. Even after his confirmation, Wilson continued to believe privately that the divestiture was unnecessary. As he wrote to a friend, there "was really no need to sell [the General Motors] stock, as the secretary never deals directly with the company in charge. The problem was mainly a political and public relations one, rather than a factual or legal one." WA, MSS Box 42, Wilson to Lawrence P. Fisher, 3 February 1953.
29. Eisenhower, *Mandate for Change,* p. 112.
30. Statement and testimony by Secretary-designate Humphrey before the Senate Finance Committee in Nathaniel Howard, ed., *The Basic Papers of George M. Humphrey,* pp. 5–9.
31. Ibid., pp. 18–23, 21. Humphrey became an advocate within the administration for construction of the seaway, however. It is, of course, open to question whether he supported the project because of its potential impact upon the nation's economy or upon the companies in which he remained interested. See Donovan, *Eisenhower,* pp. 76–77; Carleton Mabee, *The Seaway Story* (New York: Macmillan, 1961), p. 161; Gary W. Reichard, *The Reaffirmation of Republicanism,* p. 167n.
32. Howard, ed., *Basic Papers of George M. Humphrey,* p. 14.
33. Parmet, *Eisenhower and the American Crusades,* p. 179; Eisenhower, *Mandate for Change,* p. 111. Wilson's resignation from General Motors and his divestiture of General Motors stock cost him roughly $2,500,000 in lost salary, stock dividends, and appreciation, and future benefits (*Detroit News,* 28 November 1954; *New York Times,* 29 November 1954).

CHAPTER FOUR

1. *New York Times,* 12 February 1953.
2. Schilling, Hammond, and Snyder, *Strategy, Politics, and Defense Budgets,* pp. 410–12; Kolodziej, *Uncommon Defense,* pp. 89–167.
3. *New York Times,* 26 September 1952.
4. Patterson, *Mr. Republican,* p. 590.
5. Charles J. V. Murphy, "The Eisenhower Shift," pp. 86–87, 206–8; *Washington Daily News,* 16 February 1953.
6. Charles J. V. Murphy, "The Pentagon and the Korean Shell Shortage," pp. 93–94, 212; *Chicago Tribune,* 6 March 1953.
7. Senate Committee on Armed Services, *Ammunition Supplies in the Far East,* 83d Cong., 1st sess., 1953, pp. 1–2.
8. See the *Congressional Quarterly Almanac* 9 (1953): 276–77.
9. *New York Times,* 20 February 1953.
10. Rockefeller's influence on Eisenhower defense policy was especially significant during the early months of the administration. See Parmet, *Eisenhower and the American Crusades,* pp. 361–62; Roherty, *Decisions of Robert S. McNamara,* p. 47; Eisenhower, *Mandate for Change,* p. 147.
11. Duncan Norton-Taylor, "The Wilson Pentagon," pp. 222–26. Wilson's appointments included: Donald Quarles, research and development; Frank Newberry, applications engineering; Thomas Pike, supply and logistics; Franklin Floete, property and installations; Frederick Seaton, legislative and public affairs; and Dr. Melvin Casberg, health and medical affairs. Also serving on Wilson's staff at the time were: Wilfred J. McNeil, comptroller; Frank Nash, international security affairs; and John Hannah, manpower and personnel.
12. H. Struve Hensel was Wilson's choice as the department's general counsel. See *New York Times,* 17 May 1953; H. Struve Hensel, "Changes inside the Pentagon," pp. 98–108.
13. For the provisions of Reorganization Plan 6, see the *Congressional Quarterly Almanac* 9 (1953): 293–94; see also Hammond, *Organizing for Defense,* pp. 262–66; and Hensel, "Changes inside the Pentagon," pp. 107–8.
14. Millis, Mansfield, and Stein, *Arms and the State,* pp. 385–86. The Army and National Guard were vigorous rivals, chiefly due to differences over the administration of a national reserve program.
15. *Congressional Quarterly Almanac* 9 (1953): 293–94.
16. Norton-Taylor, "Wilson Pentagon," p. 96; Roherty, *Decisions of Robert S. McNamara,* p. 49; *Business Week,* 9 May 1953, p. 30.
17. Hensel, "Changes inside the Pentagon," p. 106.
18. Hoopes, *Devil and John Foster Dulles,* pp. 194–96.
19. Halberstam, *Best and the Brightest,* pp. 137–38.
20. Hammond, Schilling, and Snyder, *Strategy, Politics, and Defense Budgets,* p. 412.
21. Donovan, *Eisenhower,* p. 325.
22. WA, MSS Box 61, Minutes of Press Conference, 20 March 1953, p. 7.
23. Hammond, Schilling, and Snyder, *Strategy, Politics, and Defense Budgets,* p. 394.
24. House Committee on Appropriations, *Department of Defense Appropria-*

tions, Hearings before a Subcommittee of the Committee on Appropriations on H.R. 5969, 83d Cong., 1st sess., 1953, pp. 2–5.

25. An especially crucial factor in military programming, "lead time" refers to the elapsed time between the awarding of a military contract and the time when the contractor delivered the final product.

26. *Washington Post,* 13 March 1953; *New York Times,* 13 March 1953.

27. WA, MSS Box 61, Minutes of Press Conference, 20 March 1953, p. 7.

28. For the actual funding levels of the interim budget in comparison with the requests by the armed forces, Truman's recommendations, and Eisenhower's eventual proposal, see Kolodziej, *Uncommon Defense,* p. 169; and Hammond, Schilling, and Snyder, *Strategy, Politics, and Defense Budgets,* pp. 393–400.

29. House Committee on Appropriations, *Department of Defense Appropriations,* 1953, pp. 325–30.

30. Kinnard, *President Eisenhower and Strategy Management,* pp. 29–30.

31. Because it had recently become an independent branch of the armed services, the Air Force lacked the managerial and structural competence in 1953 to handle large-scale production and procurement programs without waste (Interview, Wilfred J. McNeil, 28 January 1978; see also WA, MSS Box 61, Minutes of Press Conference, 20 March 1953, pp. 7–10).

32. WA, MSS Box 61, Minutes of Press Conference, 20 March 1953, p. 10.

33. George Kistiakowsky, *Scientist at the White House,* pp. xxxvi, lv; Interview, Carey A. Randall, 2 February 1978; see also Borklund, *Men of the Pentagon,* pp. 143–44.

34. WA, "Addresses by C. E. Wilson," 1953, Address by Secretary of Defense Charles E. Wilson at the Armed Forces Day Dinner, the Statler Hotel, Washington, D.C., 15 May 1953, p. 6.

35. Donovan, *Eisenhower,* pp. 53–54; *Washington Post,* 21 May 1953. Yorty was the first legislator to call for Wilson's resignation. Over the next four years, many other senators and congressmen demanded Wilson's resignation after controversial policy decisions.

36. *Washington Post,* 26 May 1953.

37. *New York Times,* 5 June 1953; Kolodziej, *Uncommon Defense,* pp. 172–73.

38. Wilson's unhappiness at Vandenberg was not publicly revealed until several weeks later. See *Chicago Tribune,* 23 June 1953.

39. Senate Committee on Appropriations, 83d Cong., 1st sess., *Hearings before the Subcommittee on Defense Appropriations,* pp. 435–39.

40. Ibid., pp. 435–38, 478.

41. *Congressional Record,* 83d Cong., 1st sess., 1953, pp. 9462–65.

42. *New York Times,* 2 July 1953.

43. For a brief discussion of the debate over the interim budget, see Kolodziej, *Uncommon Defense,* pp. 171–79.

44. Charles E. Wilson, "We Are Changing Our Strategy," pp. 34–35.

CHAPTER FIVE

1. The literature on the McCarthy period is already substantial and continues to grow. See, for example, Fred J. Cook, *The Nightmare Decade;*

Robert Griffith, *The Politics of Fear;* Richard Rovere, *Senator Joe McCarthy;* and Athan Theoharis, *Seeds of Repression.* A good recent study is Richard M. Fried, *Men against McCarthy.*

2. Acheson explained his view of McCarthy and the Republican right in *Present at the Creation,* pp. 364–69. A discussion of McCarthy's attacks on Acheson may be found in Rovere, *Senator Joe McCarthy,* pp. 12–14.

3. Cabell Phillips, *The Truman Presidency,* p. 393; Rovere, *Senator Joe McCarthy,* pp. 170–79.

4. Merle Miller, *Plain Speaking,* p. 421.

5. Hughes, *Ordeal of Power,* pp. 88–92.

6. Nixon, *Six Crises,* p. 125. Shortly after the Republicans agreed on their Eisenhower-Nixon ticket at the 1952 national convention in Chicago, a reporter asked McCarthy if he endorsed the party's choice. "I think Dick Nixon will make a fine Vice President," the senator replied (Lyon, *Eisenhower,* p. 447).

7. Hoopes, *Devil and John Foster Dulles,* pp. 5, 6, 150–53.

8. WA, MSS Box 62, Minutes of Press Conference, 4 March 1954, p. 9; WA, "Addresses by C. E. Wilson," 1954, Address by Secretary of Defense Charles E. Wilson to the Annual Convention of the Chamber of Commerce, the Statler Hotel, Washington, D.C., 26 April 1954, p. 6.

9. Donovan, *Eisenhower,* p. 294; Eisenhower, *Mandate for Change,* pp. 310–11; Parmet, *Eisenhower and the American Crusades,* pp. 342–44.

10. Eisenhower, *Mandate for Change,* p. 310.

11. Lyon, *Eisenhower,* pp. 569–73.

12. Eisenhower, *Mandate for Change,* p. 311.

13. Lyon, *Eisenhower,* p. 571.

14. Parmet, *Eisenhower and the American Crusades,* p. 344. The review board voted two to one against Oppenheimer, with Evans being his lone supporter. The Atomic Energy Commission upheld that decision, four to one.

15. David E. Lilienthal, *The Journal of David E. Lilienthal,* vol. 3, *Venturesome Years, 1950–1955,* pp. 510–11; Strauss, *Men and Decisions,* p. 295; Eisenhower, *Mandate for Change,* p. 313.

16. WA, MSS Box 62, Minutes of Press Conference, 14 April 1954, p. 4; Minutes of Press Conference, 18 April 1954, p. 4.

17. For a full discussion on the Oppenheimer loyalty review, see John Major, *The Oppenheimer Hearings.*

18. Eisenhower, *Mandate for Change,* p. 322.

19. Parmet, *Eisenhower and the American Crusades,* p. 346.

20. Eisenhower, *Mandate for Change,* p. 323. The only possible administrative error committed by the Army was its failure to learn of Peress's membership in the American Labor party until after his induction. The promotion and discharge complied with Army procedures, although McCarthy demanded that Peress be court-martialed. A court-martial, however, was legally impossible after an honorable discharge; furthermore, there were no grounds for one.

21. Ibid., p. 323.

22. Parmet, *Eisenhower and the American Crusades,* p. 347; WA, MSS Box 62, Minutes of Press Conference, 4 March 1954, p. 2.
23. Donovan, *Eisenhower,* pp. 250–51; Griffith, *Politics of Fear,* p. 247; Parmet, *Eisenhower and the American Crusades,* pp. 346–47.
24. Parmet, *Eisenhower and the American Crusades,* p. 347.
25. Ibid., p. 351.
26. WA, MSS Box 62, Minutes of Press Conference, 4 March 1954, pp. 4, 7, 8. There was speculation that McCarthy and his chief assistant, Roy Cohn, had pressured Stevens and other Army personnel into giving preferential treatment to Schine, who was then stationed at Fort Dix, New Jersey. Drew Pearson, the syndicated columnist, first published such a story in mid-December. One week later, the *Baltimore Sun* ran a series of follow-up articles on the subject. In late January, the *New York Post* followed suit. In February, calls began for a congressional investigation of McCarthy's alleged actions on Schine's behalf. See Griffith, *Politics of Fear,* pp. 245–46; Lately Thomas, *When Even Angels Wept,* pp. 478–80.
27. Parmet, *Eisenhower and the American Crusades,* p. 353.
28. *New York Times,* 11 March 1954.
29. On 9 February 1954, the United States Court of Appeals rendered a decision in the case of *Nelson* v. *Peckham* which had direct bearing on the Peress case and Department of Defense security procedures. Dr. Roger Nelson, a dentist, was called to military service under the Doctor Draft Act. Upon application for a commission pursuant to this law, Dr. Nelson declined to answer the questions on the loyalty questionnaire, claiming his rights to remain silent under the Fifth Amendment. He was denied a commission and drafted as an enlisted man. Later he decided that he would no longer claim the Fifth Amendment and stated on his loyalty form that he had former affiliations with the Communist party and the Young Communist League and was still a member of the International Workers Order. His commission was denied and the court ruled that, in accordance with the Doctor Draft Act, Nelson was either to be granted a commission or released. See Senate Committee on Armed Services, 83d Cong., 2d sess., *Amendments to the Doctor Draft Act,* 1954, pp. 1–4.
30. Ibid., pp. 3–5.
31. Ibid., pp. 23–26, 27–28, 29, 42–46, 49–56.
32. WA, "Addresses by C. E. Wilson," 1954, Department of Defense Memorandum by Secretary of Defense Charles E. Wilson, pp. 773–78.
33. Senate Committee on Armed Services, *Amendments to the Doctor Draft Act,* 1954, p. 149.
34. Ibid., pp. 151–52, 153–56.
35. *Congress and the Nation,* p. 277.
36. Cook, *Nightmare Decade,* pp. 509–11; Rovere, *Senator Joe McCarthy,* pp. 215–18.
37. *Christian Science Monitor,* 18 March 1954.
38. WA, MSS Box 62, Press Interview, 11 May 1954, p. 3.
39. Cook, *Nightmare Decade,* p. 490.
40. WA, MSS Box 62, Minutes of Press Conference, 21 April 1954, p. 4.

41. Eisenhower, *Mandate for Change,* pp. 597, 328.
42. WA, MSS Box 62, Minutes of Press Conference, 10 August 1954, p. 10.
43. Address by Charles E. Wilson to the National Convention of the Chamber of Commerce, p. 15.
44. Cook, *Nightmare Decade,* pp. 440–42; Hughes, *Ordeal of Power,* pp. 88–96; Lyon, *Eisenhower,* pp. 571–73; Parmet, *Eisenhower and the American Crusades,* pp. 266–67.

CHAPTER SIX

1. Hoopes, *Devil and John Foster Dulles,* p. 195; Kinnard, *President Eisenhower and Strategy Management,* p. 24. See also Charles J. V. Murphy, "Is the H-Bomb Enough?," pp. 102–3.
2. Kolodziej, *Uncommon Defense,* pp. 194–95.
3. Hoopes, *Devil and John Foster Dulles,* p. 196.
4. Hughes, *Living Presidency,* pp. 15–16; *Ordeal of Power,* pp. 103–4.
5. *Detroit News,* 11 October 1954.
6. Ambrose, *Rise to Globalism,* p. 241. The liberal columnist I. F. Stone noted: "It was through Eisenhower that the big businessmen in the Cabinet like Humphrey and Wilson have been able to put some brake on the arms race" (*The Haunted Fifties* [New York: Random House, 1963], p. 106).
7. Hoopes, *Devil and John Foster Dulles,* pp. 197–201. Hoopes was critical of Dulles's apparent lack of knowledge about strategic matters: "It was characteristic of his approach that he did not often find it necessary to think about military matters beyond the problem of devising and issuing political warnings" (p. 197).
8. LaFeber, *America, Russia, and the Cold War,* p. 196. Many historians, most notably Ambrose and LaFeber, are now contending that Eisenhower wanted a lessening of tensions with the Soviet Union. If such an interpretation is accurate, then Dulles's hard-line statements may be viewed more as symbolic gestures than as statements of policy. See Ambrose, *Rise to Globalism,* pp. 241–45; LaFeber, *America, Russia, and the Cold War,* pp. 128–98.
9. Kinnard, *President Eisenhower and Strategy Management,* pp. 8, 10, 124.
10. House Committee on Appropriations, *Department of Defense Appropriations, Hearings before the Subcommittee on Defense Appropriations,* 83d Cong., 2d sess., 1954, pp. 3–5. Wilson remained somewhat suspicious of the concept of "unification," once telling an interviewer that one result of unification might have been a "concentration of stupidity" (*U.S. News and World Report,* 11 October 1957, p. 34). See also Wilson, "We Are Changing Our Strategy," p. 35; WA, Wilson Address to Bull Elephants Club, 1 April 1954.
11. Senate Committee on Appropriations, *Department of Defense Appropriations,* 1954, pp. 4–5, 8–9, 15–16.
12. Ibid., pp. 6–7.
13. Ibid., pp. 20–24, 37–38.
14. *Congressional Record,* 83d Cong., 2d sess., 1954, pp. 8321–48.

15. *Congress and the Nation,* p. 280; *Congressional Quarterly Almanac, 1954,* p. 156; Kolodziej, *Uncommon Defense,* pp. 180–213.
16. For a specific detailed discussion of the Senate debate on the fiscal year 1955 defense budget, see Hammond, Schilling, and Snyder, *Strategy, Politics, and Defense Budgets,* pp. 418–40; Kinnard, *President Eisenhower and Strategy Management,* pp. 30–36; and Kolodziej, *Uncommon Defense,* pp. 180–213.
17. Wilson may have been partially to blame for Ferguson's defeat. On 11 October, Wilson spoke at a press conference in Detroit, where he defended himself against charges by Senator Henry Jackson that he had been showing favoritism in awarding some defense contracts to General Motors, although he had only been following through on some agreements made during the Truman years. Many Democrats felt that defense contracts should be awarded to industries in areas of high unemployment, but Wilson maintained that contracts must be awarded to industries with the appropriate technology; the unemployment rate in the area should be a secondary consideration. In answer to a question, Wilson stated that he "had a lot of sympathy for the jobless in labor surplus areas but that he always respected bird dogs more than kennel dogs, you know, one who'll go out and hunt for food, rather than sit on his fanny and yelp." This remark cost the Republicans politically. Walter Reuther, the president of the United Auto Workers, immediately called for Wilson's resignation. Some Republicans, most notably Governor William Stratton of Illinois, tried to avoid public appearances with Wilson when he visited their area. See *Detroit News,* 11 October, 1954; *Chicago Tribune,* 13 October 1954.
18. WA, letter by Secretary of Defense Charles E. Wilson to President Dwight D. Eisenhower, 3 January 1955, in "Addresses by C. E. Wilson," 1955, p. 6.
19. Ibid., President Dwight D. Eisenhower to Secretary of Defense Charles E. Wilson, 5 January 1955, pp. 7–10.
20. See, for example, WA, MSS Box 71, Address by Secretary of Defense Charles E. Wilson at the Sixth Annual Armed Forces Day Dinner, Sheraton-Park Hotel, Washington, D.C., 20 May 1955.
21. Kolodziej, *Uncommon Defense,* pp. 214–19.
22. *New York Times,* 10 February 1955. According to the administration's estimates, the Army would be reduced from 1,407,000 men in fiscal year 1955 to 1,172,000 in fiscal year 1956.
23. Senate Committee on Appropriations, *Department of Defense Appropriations,* 84th Cong., 1st sess., 1955, pp. 7–11, 13, 15.
24. *Congress and the Nation,* p. 285; Charles J. V. Murphy, "New Air Situation," pp. 85–86, 218, 221, 224, 226, 230. Symington's charge was preliminary to his more vigorous opposition in 1956 to the administration's air power program. See chapter 6, below.
25. Symington, along with some other administration critics, seemed to be influenced by reports of a flight demonstration of Soviet aircraft in Moscow on Aviation Day in the spring of 1955, where the Russians dis-

played their newly developed heavy bomber. The Soviets gave the impression that their production of heavy aircraft had increased dramatically. In reality (according to the Central Intelligence Agency's explanation), the Russians had merely repeated overflights of a ten-aircraft squadron (Allen Dulles, *The Craft of Intelligence,* p. 149; Kinnard, *President Eisenhower and Strategy Management,* p. 39). Wilson later speculated that the Russians were reenacting a 1950s version of the Potemkin Village trick, when in 1787, Prince Gregory Potemkin built a series of "towns" to impress Catherine the Great on her tour of the Crimea. Actually, Potemkin built no towns, only false fronts on buildings. The administration was not as concerned as its critics about the Soviet air buildup (Murphy, "New Air Situation," p. 218).

26. Senate Committee on Appropriations, *Department of Defense Appropriations, Hearings before a Subcommittee of the Committee on Appropriations on H.R. 6042,* 84th Cong., 1st sess., 1955, pp. 1426–28, 1432–40, 1440–41.
27. *Congress and the Nation,* p. 286.
28. Eisenhower, *Mandate for Change,* pp. 454–55; Halberstam, *Best and the Brightest,* pp. 472–74.
29. Halberstam, *Best and the Brightest,* pp. 142–44; Huntington, *Common Defense,* p. 84; Matthew B. Ridgway, *Soldier,* p. 316.
30. James Tobin, "The Eisenhower Economy and National Security," pp. 323, 324, 329.
31. Eisenhower, *Mandate for Change,* pp. 446–48.

CHAPTER SEVEN

1. House Committee on Appropriations, *Department of Defense Appropriations,* 84th Cong., 2d sess., 1956, pp. 1–3. The Army's budgetary allotment for fiscal year 1957 was $7.8 billion, over $2 billion less than the Navy's $10 billion and roughly half of the Air Force's $15.7 billion.
2. Alexander, *Holding the Line,* p. 70; Kinnard, *President Eisenhower and Strategy Management,* p. 48.
3. Ridgway, *Soldier,* pp. 317–21. Wilson discussed his relationship with Ridgway during a press conference in early 1956 (WA, MSS Box 63, Minutes of Press Conference, 17 January 1956, pp. 1–3).
4. Halberstam, *Best and the Brightest,* p. 472.
5. Maxwell D. Taylor, *Swords and Plowshares,* p. 137. See also Maxwell D. Taylor, *The Uncertain Trumpet,* pp. 28–29; Halberstam, *Best and the Brightest,* p. 473.
6. Alexander, *Holding the Line,* p. 70; Kinnard, *President Eisenhower and Strategy Management,* pp. 49–50.
7. Statement attributed to General Curtis LeMay, commander of the Strategic Air Command (*Congressional Quarterly Almanac, 1956,* pp. 609, 613).
8. WA, MSS Box 61, Statement to the Senate Armed Services Committee, 12 January 1956, pp. 1–4; Donovan, *Eisenhower,* pp. 329–30; Kolodziej, *Uncommon Defense,* pp. 226–30.
9. Matthew B. Ridgway, "Keep the Army out of Politics," *Saturday Evening Post,* 28 January 1956, pp. 34–35, 72. See also Ridgway, *Soldier,* pp. 274,

292. See *Washington Evening Star*, 28 January 1956, for a critique of Ridgway's charges.

10. WA, MSS Box 69, Minutes of Press Conference, 17 January 1956, pp. 2–3.

11. *New York Times*, 20 January 1953.

12. Kinnard, *President Eisenhower and Strategy Management*, pp. 50, 54.

13. *New York Times*, 20 January 1956. Symington was responding to the *Post* excerpt entitled "Conflict in the Pentagon," in which Ridgway charged that the administration did not formulate defense policy on the basis of sound military judgment, but was too strongly influenced by political factors (*Saturday Evening Post*, 21 January 1956, pp. 46, 48).

14. *Washington Evening Star*, 25 January 1956. Wilson's supporters in Congress did speak out in his favor, however. When Wilson testified on 24 January to the House Subcommittee on Defense Appropriations, Gerald Ford of Michigan told him that Ridgway's criticism was "unfortunate" and "unfounded." Ford commended Wilson for his concern for American servicemen (House Committee on Appropriations, *Department of Defense Appropriations, Hearings before the Subcommittee on Defense Appropriations*, 84th Cong., 2d sess., 1956, p. 64).

15. WA, MSS Box 69, Minutes of Press Conference, 1 February 1956, p. 37.

16. Donovan, *Eisenhower*, p. 330; Kinnard, *President Eisenhower and Strategy Management*, p. 50; Kolodziej, *Uncommon Defense*, pp. 233–36.

17. WA, MSS Box 69, Minutes of Press Conference, 6 March 1956, pp. 9, 12, 25.

18. WA, Address by C. E. Wilson to the National Press Club, 13 March 1956, p. 8; *New York Times*, 14 March 1956.

19. *Chicago Tribune*, 30 March 1956.

20. Kinnard, *President Eisenhower and Strategy Management*, pp. 50–53.

21. Donovan, *Eisenhower*, p. 330.

22. Senate Committee on Appropriations, *Department of Defense Appropriations*, 1956, p. 4.

23. Ibid., p. 22. Wilson repeated this view on 14 May before the Senate Foreign Relations Committee. See Senate Committee on Foreign Relations, *Mutual Security*, 84th Cong., 2d sess., 1956, pp. 555–56, 564, 630.

24. See *Time*, 4 June 1956, for an analysis of the interservice rivalry which broke fully into view in late May 1956.

25. Halberstam, *Best and the Brightest*, pp. 474–76.

26. *Time*, 4 June 1956, pp. 19–22. Colonel Scott, the author of *God Is My Co-Pilot*, was a past member of the Flying Tiger squadrons which served in the China-Burma-India theater during World War II under General Claire Chennault. An elaborate propagandist of the Air Force and a vigorous detractor of the Army, Scott was well qualified to handle the Air Force's public relations. For Scott's experience in the Air Force, see Barbara W. Tuchman, *Stilwell and the American Experience in China, 1911–1945*, pp. 374–75, 430.

27. *Time*, 4 June 1956. Leviero, himself an Army Reserve officer, was a skilled reporter who won a Pulitzer Prize for his coverage of Truman-MacArthur conference on Wake Island in October 1950.

28. Wilson was quoted as saying, "There's a bunch of eager beavers out there and if they stick their necks out again, I'll chop them off" (Halberstam, *Best and the Brightest*, p. 476).
29. WA, MSS Box 69, Minutes of Press Conference, 21 May 1956, pp. 1-4.
30. Ibid., pp. 16, 23-27.
31. Halberstam, *Best and the Brightest*, pp. 476-77. Wilson's action must have been particularly distasteful for Taylor. Both *The Uncertain Trumpet* and *Swords and Plowshares* criticize Wilson but make no mention of this incident.
32. *Congressional Quarterly Almanac, 1956*, p. 613.
33. Kolodziej, *Uncommon Defense*, pp. 233-36.
34. WA, MSS Box 191, "Present and Planned Strength of the United States Air Force."
35. Kolodziej, *Uncommon Defense*, p. 236.
36. The difference in proposals for increases in appropriations ranged from the Senate Appropriation Committee's request of an additional $1.6 billion to General LeMay's $3.8 billion. Had Congress followed LeMay's proposal, the Air Force would have been forced to let contracts two or three years in advance of actual delivery (Interview, Wilfred J. McNeil, 23 January 1978).
37. WA, MSS Box 69, Minutes of Press Conference, Quantico, Virginia, 21 June 1956, p. 1-4.
38. Ibid., p. 18.
39. *Congressional Record,* 84th Cong., 2d sess., 1956, pp. 10814-17.
40. Ibid., pp. 10971-72. Russell's charges were not true, especially in regard to Wilson's alleged intimidation of military leaders and to his keeping them from fully advising the Congress. Previous testimony by members of the Joint Chiefs before the Senate Armed Services Committee showed that the military leadership was allowed to present its professional judgment about the defense program. Ridgway even admitted that "actions which in my view were detrimental to the strength and spirit of the army I protested in meetings with the Joint Chiefs; in my testimony before committees of Congress; and by letter and in personal conferences with the Secretary of Defense" (*Soldier*, p. 274).
41. *Congressional Quarterly Almanac, 1956*, p. 615.
42. *New York Times,* 29 June 1956. The subcommittee included Symington, Ervin, Jackson, Saltonstall, and James Duff (R.-Pa.).
43. Senate Committee on Armed Services, *Study of Airpower, Hearings before the Subcommittee on the Air Force of the Committee on Armed Services,* 84th Cong., 2d sess., 1956, pp. 1659-63. See also *Chicago Tribune,* 30 June 1956.
44. Senate Committee on Armed Services, *Airpower,* pp. 1691, 1778-79.
45. Ibid., pp. 1789-90.
46. *Washington Post,* 4 July 1956. The subcommittee issued its full report in February 1957. The majority opinion stated that the administration's air power program was rife with mismanagement, and as a result the nation had been weakened. The minority opinion supported Wilson's analysis of

American air superiority over the Soviets and criticized the majority's conclusions for their lack of objectivity. For summaries, see *Congressional Quarterly Almanac, 1957*, p. 132. Wilson replied to Symington's conclusions in a letter dated 18 July 1956.

Dear Mr. Chairman:

Shortly before the conclusion of your hearings on July 3rd, you read a statement into the record which you said represented your personal views regarding my testimony and in which you pointed out that there were inconsistencies between my sworn testimony and that of other witnesses. At that time, I requested permission to reply to your statement.

After a careful review of my testimony, and that of others, I must state that I disagree with the conclusions in your statement. I call your attention to the prepared statement which I made before the committee on June 29th and my testimony which gave the facts as known to me and represent my views.

There are two matters which I think it would be helpful to clarify for the benefit of the American people. The first relates to my intentions with respect to the additional funds appropriated by Congress for the Air Force. I stated at the hearing, and now repeat, I do not propose to impound the funds and I propose to carry out the intent of Congress, subject to the limiting factors proposed by Congress itself and to the recommendations of the Secretary of the Air Force and to my own best judgment as to the security needs of the nation.

The second point relates to the relative airpower of the United States vis-a-vis Russia. Depending on how such a question is phrased any of a number of assumptions could be proven by the best intelligence available. I merely wish to emphasize my belief, based on the facts, that in our overall air strength we are ahead of the Russians today and we intend in the future to build and maintain total air strength capable of preserving the security of the United States, and as a visible deterrent to wars of any kind.

The military problems which have been investigated by your committee are extremely complicated. In forming any judgement as to their solution, I have endeavored to study all relevant data and to secure the advice and opinions of the most highly qualified experts our country can provide. In some cases my advisors have not been in complete agreement. My decisions and my recommendations to the President and the Congress have been thought out to the best of my ability and have always been based on what I considered to be in the best interest of national security.

You express concern that my sworn testimony was at variance with that of some of the officers who testified before your committee. While, in my opinion, my testimony and theirs is in general accord as to facts, it certainly does not surprise me that differences of opinion have developed. In fact, I consider it normal for divergent opinions to exist whenever individuals express their honest views on complicated and important matters and have different degrees of responsibility.

When all the testimony has been released, I trust that the true facts regarding our military strength, particularly as to airpower, will have been fully presented in proper perspective to the American people.

(WA, "Addresses by C. E. Wilson," 1956, pp. 968–70.)

The question remains of why Symington waited until February 1957 to release his report. In _Stuart Symington,_ Paul I. Wellman states that the senator did not want the report released in 1956 because it could have been viewed as a partisan gesture during an election year (p. 194). That interpretation assumes that Symington's analysis was correct. If the "bomber gap" of 1956 was fictitious, any attempt by the Democrats to use it as an issue against Eisenhower, who possessed the intelligence estimates of Soviet air strength, could have backfired badly.

47. _Congress and the Nation,_ p. 292.
48. WA, "Addresses by C. E. Wilson," 1956, Transcript of "Face the Nation," 28 October 1956, p. 1098.
49. See "900 Million Dollar Bobble," _U.S. News and World Report,_ 8 March 1957, pp. 56–59.

CHAPTER EIGHT

1. Hughes, _Ordeal of Power,_ pp. 76–77.
2. Wilson held sixty-nine formal press conferences while serving as secretary of defense and met informally with the press at least fifty other times. See _Washington Daily News,_ 2 February 1957.
3. See "Administration's National Reserve Plan," _Congressional Digest_ (April 1955), pp. 104–5.
4. See "Present National Guard Program," _Congressional Quarterly,_ 7 February 1957, p. 179.
5. Ibid., p. 157. See also Martha Derthick, "Militia Lobby in the Missile Age: The Politics of the National Guard," in Samuel P. Huntington, ed., _Changing Patterns of Military Politics,_ p. 228.
6. _New York Times,_ 29 January 1957.
7. _Congressional Digest_ (April 1955), p. 99.
8. _New York Times,_ 29, 30 January 1957; _Baltimore Sun,_ 29 January 1957; _Detroit News,_ 29 January 1957.
9. _New York Times,_ 30 January 1957; _Christian Science Monitor,_ 29 January 1957; _Washington Post,_ 29 January 1957.
10. _Congressional Record,_ 85th Cong., 1st sess., 1957, pp. 1394–1400.
11. _Baltimore Sun,_ 29 January 1957; U.S. Congress, Senate, _Congressional Record,_ 85th Cong., 1st sess., p. 1396.
12. _Chicago Tribune,_ 30 January 1957.
13. _New York Times,_ 30 January 1957. Wilson was not in fact referring to the White House itself as a "dunghill," although one could understandably reach that conclusion. He was alluding to the Roman philosopher Seneca's aphorism, "Every cock is at his best on his own dunghill." Wilson's "dunghill" would have been the Pentagon.
14. Ibid., 31 January, 5 February 1957.
15. _Washington Post,_ 31 January 1957; _Washington Star,_ 31 January 1957.
16. For a full profile of the Wilson family, see _Chicago Tribune,_ 6 February 1957.
17. WA, MSS Boxes 77, 78, and 79, "Letters re: National Guard." The total exceeded 1,400, with many letters coming from registered Democratic

voters who differed with the administration's defense policy but admired Wilson for his candor about the National Guard. Many also praised Mrs. Wilson and the secretary tried to respond through his office to each letter.

18. WA, MSS Box 76, James T. Williams to Charles E. Wilson, 1 February 1957; Ernest Dale to Charles E. Wilson, 1 February 1957.
19. WA, MSS Box 76. Examples included "Join the Guard and Avoid the Draft," *Sacramento Citizen News*, 29 January 1957; and "Only 60 Days Left to Avoid the Draft," *Houston Chronicle*, 30 January 1957.
20. WA, MSS Box 76, David K. Jameson to Charles E. Wilson, 29 January 1957; Mrs. G. Fohlen to Charles E. Wilson, 29 January 1957.
21. *Washington Post*, 4 February 1957.
22. *New York Times*, 4 February 1957. See also *Congressional Record*, 85th Cong., 1st sess., 1957, p. 1991.
23. The campaign involved letters to congressmen, state governors, and legislators. The *National Guardsman* of March 1957 contained an attack on Wilson's policies (pp. 14–17, 30).
24. *New York Times*, 19 February 1957.
25. Ibid.
26. *New York Herald Tribune*, 21 February 1957.
27. Robert W. Smith, associate editor of the *Minneapolis Star*, wrote editorials against Walsh's position and sent copies to Wilson (WA, News File, *Minneapolis Star*, 4, 8, 22 February 1957; see also *Minneapolis Tribune*, 4, 8, 22 February 1957). Smith's correspondence with Wilson may be found in WA, MSS Box 76, Robert W. Smith to Charles E. Wilson, 1 March 1957.
28. *Philadelphia Evening Bulletin*, 23 February 1957.
29. *New York Times*, 24 February 1957.
30. Martha Derthick, *The National Guard in Politics*, pp. 138–39.
31. *New York Herald Tribune*, 24 February 1957.
32. WA, MSS Box 76, Charles E. Wilson to Carl Kindl, 2 March 1957.

CHAPTER NINE

1. Samuel P. Huntington, *The Soldier and the State*, pp. 442–43; Interview, Thomas S. Gates, 2 February 1978.
2. Charles J. V. Murphy, "Strategy Overtakes Mr. Wilson," pp. 80–81; Borklund, *Men of the Pentagon*, p. 155.
3. Interview, Wilfred J. McNeil, 23 January 1978; Borklund, *Department of Defense*, pp. 122–23; Borklund, *Men of the Pentagon*, pp. 154–55; *New York World Telegram*, 15 October 1955; Kinnard, *President Eisenhower and Strategy Management*, p. 127.
4. Interview, Wilfred J. McNeil; Interview, Thomas S. Gates; Interview, John A. Hannah, 20 October 1978; Roherty, *Decisions of Robert S. McNamara*, p. 49.
5. Hammond, *Organizing for Defense*, p. 294; Millis, Mansfield, and Stein, *Arms and the State*, pp. 382–83.
6. Interview, Wilfred J. McNeil. See also interview with Wilson in *U.S. News and World Report*, 30 December 1949, pp. 33–34.

7. WA, MSS Box 50, Charles E. Wilson to Alfred P. Sloan, 17 January 1955.
8. Millis, Mansfield, and Stein, *Arms and the State,* p. 382. See also chapter 3, above.
9. Norton-Taylor, "Wilson Pentagon," pp. 222, 224; *New York Times,* 17 May 1953.
10. *U.S. News and World Report,* 30 December 1949, p. 30; WA, MSS Box 50, Wilson to Sloan, 17 January 1955.
11. Interview, Wilfred J. McNeil, *Business Week,* 9 May 1953; Norton-Taylor, "Wilson Pentagon," p. 96; Hensel, "Changes inside the Pentagon," p. 100. See Hensel for a summary of the rationale for and evolution of the Defense Department's concept of decentralized administration.
12. *U.S. News and World Report,* 18 October 1957, p. 84.
13. Two fine studies discuss the impact of Wilson's decision to allow competition between the armed services for the development of weapons systems: Michael H. Armacost, *The Politics of Weapons Innovation;* and Edmund Beard, *Developing the ICBM.* See also Borklund, *Men of the Pentagon,* p. 156; *Newsweek,* 8 December 1952, p. 22.
14. Interview, Wilfred J. McNeil.
15. Interview, John A. Hannah; Smith, "Secretary Wilson's Year of Trial," p. 19.
16. Ridgway, *Soldier,* p. 283; Taylor, *Uncertain Trumpet,* pp. 28–29; Interview, Wilfred J. McNeil; Interview, Carey A. Randall; Interview, Thomas S. Gates.
17. Interview, Carey A. Randall; Interview, John A. Hannah. See also WA, MSS Box 50, Charles E. Wilson to Alfred P. Sloan, 17 January 1955, p. 21.
18. WA, MSS Box 50, Outline of General Motors Dual Purpose Plants. See also *Newsweek,* 8 December 1952.
19. Norton-Taylor, "Wilson Pentagon," p. 96.
20. Interview, Wilfred J. McNeil; Huntington, *Soldier and the State,* pp. 394–95.
21. Kinnard, *President Eisenhower and Strategy Management,* p. 127; Interview, Wilfred J. McNeil.
22. *U.S. News and World Report,* 18 October 1957, p. 88.
23. James J. Gavin, *War and Peace in the Space Age,* p. 155; WA, MSS Box 61, Minutes of Press Conference, 20 November 1953, p. 9.
24. Hughes, *Ordeal of Power,* p. 138; Charles J. V. Murphy, "The Budget—and Eisenhower," p. 228.
25. WA, "Addresses by C. E. Wilson," 1956, Address to National Press Club, 13 March 1956, Washington, D.C., pp. 10–12.
26. Murphy, "Budget—and Eisenhower," pp. 96, 228.
27. Senate Committee on Appropriations, *Hearings before the Subcommittee on Defense Appropriations,* 85th Cong., 1st sess., 1957, p. 25.
28. Adams, *Firsthand Report,* p. 404.
29. Charles J. V. Murphy, "America's Widening Military Margin," pp. 218, 220.
30. Borklund, *Men of the Pentagon,* pp. 156–60.

CHAPTER TEN

1. WA, MSS Box 63, Minutes of Press Conference, 2 October 1957, pp. 1–15.
2. Interview, Thomas S. Gates.
3. Interview, Carey A. Randall; Interview, John A. Hannah.
4. For a useful although very sympathetic appraisal of Wilson's Pentagon career, see "Well Done, Mr. Wilson," *Barron's Weekly*, 2 October 1957.
5. Gavin, *War and Peace in the Space Age*, p. 155.
6. Aliano, *American Defense Policy from Eisenhower to Kennedy*, p. 104. This statement is taken from Wilson's Senate testimony.
7. Smith, "Secretary Wilson's Year of Trial," p. 19.
8. See WA, MSS Box 62, Minutes of Press Conference, 4 May 1954, p. 13.
9. Fletcher Knebel, "Every Time He Opens His Mouth He Says Something," *Look*, 19 March 1955, pp. 125–27; WA, MSS Box 63, Minutes of Press Conference, 2 October 1957, p. 27.

Bibliography

THE Charles E. Wilson Archives, located at Anderson College, Anderson, Indiana, contain only material relating to Wilson's business and governmental career. The collection includes 202 numbered boxes of business correspondence, speeches, press releases, public statements, and transcripts of press conferences. The collection also includes a wide range of personal correspondence spanning 1926 to 1961 and a file of 22 large scrapbooks made up of newspaper clippings and photographs. Unpublished materials are numbered by page, making the task of documentation simpler. The archives were the gift of the Wilson family, who chose Anderson College as the repository for these materials because of Wilson's long association with the college and the friendships which he established with its students, faculty, and administration during the 1920s, when he managed the Remy Electric Company in Anderson.

Acheson, Dean. *Present at the Creation*. New York: Norton, 1969.

Adams, Sherman. *Firsthand Report*. New York: Harper and Bros., 1961.

Albertson, Dean, ed. *Eisenhower as President*. New York: Hill and Wang, 1963.

Alexander, Charles C. *Holding the Line: The Eisenhower Era, 1952–1961*. Bloomington, Ind.: Indiana University Press, 1975.

Aliano, Richard A. *American Defense Policy from Eisenhower to Kennedy.* Athens, Ohio: Ohio University Press, 1975.

Ambrose, Stephen E. *Rise to Globalism.* Baltimore, Md.: Penguin Books, 1972.

Armacost, Michael H. *The Politics of Weapons Innovation: The Thor-Jupiter Controversy.* New York: Columbia University Press, 1969.

Barber, James David. *The Presidential Character.* Englewood Cliffs, N.J.: Prentice-Hall, 1972.

Beard, Edmund. *Developing the ICBM: A Study in Bureaucratic Politics.* New York: Columbia University Press, 1976.

Benson, Ezra Taft. *Crossfire.* Garden City, N.Y.: Doubleday, 1962.

Blum, John M. *V Was for Victory.* New York: Harcourt, Brace, Jovanovich, 1976.

Borklund, C. W. *The Department of Defense.* New York: Praeger, 1968.

———. *Men of the Pentagon.* New York: Praeger, 1966.

Branyan, Robert L., ed. *The Eisenhower Administration, 1953–1961: A Documentary History.* New York: Random House, 1971.

Brown, John Mason. *Through These Men.* New York: Harper and Bros., 1956.

Catton, Bruce. *The War Lords of Washington.* New York: Harcourt, Brace, 1948.

Childs, Marquis. *Eisenhower: Captive Hero.* New York: Harcourt, Brace, 1958.

Cochran, Bert. *Harry S. Truman and the Crisis Presidency.* New York: Funk and Wagnalls, 1973.

Collier, Richard. *Bridge across the Sky.* New York: McGraw-Hill, 1978.

Cook, Fred J. *The Nightmare Decade.* New York: Random House, 1971.

Davies, Paul L. "A Business Look at the Army." *Harvard Business Review* 32 (July-August 1954): 55–56.

Derthick, Martha. *The National Guard in Politics.* Cambridge, Mass.: Harvard University Press, 1965.

Donovan, Robert J. *Eisenhower: The Inside Story of the First Term.* New York: Harper and Bros., 1956.

Drucker, Peter F. *Management: Tasks, Responsibilities, Practices.* New York: Harper and Row, 1974.

———. *The Unseen Revolution: How Pension Fund Socialism Came to the United States.* New York: Harper and Row, 1976.

Duffield, Eugene. "Organizing for Defense." *Harvard Business Review* 31 (September-October 1953): 29–43.

Dulles, Allen. *The Craft of Intelligence.* New York: Harper and Row, 1963.

Eisenhower, Dwight D. *Mandate for Change: The White House Years, 1953–1956.* Garden City, N.Y.: Doubleday, 1963.

―――. *Waging Peace: The White House Years, 1956–1961.* Garden City, N.Y.: Doubleday, 1965.

Feis, Herbert. *From Trust to Terror: The Onset of the Cold War, 1945– 1950.* New York: Norton, 1971.

Fried, Richard M. *Men against McCarthy.* New York: Columbia University Press, 1976.

Frier, David. *Conflict of Interest in the Eisenhower Administration.* Ames, Iowa: Iowa State University Press, 1969.

Gavin, James G. *War and Peace in the Space Age.* New York: Harper and Bros., 1958.

Goldman, Eric F. *The Crucial Decade and after, 1945–1960.* New York: Random House, 1961.

Graebner, Norman A. "Eisenhower's Popular Leadership." *Current History* 39 (October 1960): 230–36, 244.

Griffith, Robert. *The Politics of Fear.* Lexington, Ky.: University Press of Kentucky, 1970.

Halberstam, David. *The Best and the Brightest.* New York: Macmillan, 1972.

Hammond, Paul Y. *Organizing for Defense.* Princeton, N.J.: Princeton University Press, 1961.

Haynes, Richard. *The Awesome Power: Harry S. Truman as Commander in Chief.* Baton Rouge, La.: Louisiana State University Press, 1973.

Hensel, H. Struve. "Changes inside the Pentagon." *Harvard Business Review* 32 (January-February 1954): 98–108.

Hoopes, Townsend. *The Devil and John Foster Dulles.* Boston: Little, Brown, 1973.

Howard, Nathaniel, ed. *The Basic Papers of George M. Humphrey.* Cleveland, Ohio: Western Reserve Historical Society, 1965.

Hughes, Emmett John. *The Living Presidency.* New York: Coward-McCann and Geoghegan, 1972.

―――. *The Ordeal of Power.* New York: Atheneum, 1963.

Huntington, Samuel P. *The Common Defense.* New York: Columbia University Press, 1957.

―――. *The Soldier and the State.* Cambridge, Mass.: Harvard University Press, 1957.

―――, ed. *Changing Patterns of Military Politics.* New York: Free Press of Glencoe, 1962.

Kempton, Murray. "The Underestimation of Dwight D. Eisenhower." *Esquire,* September 1967, p. 108.

Kinnard, Douglas. "Eisenhower and the Defense Budget." *Journal of Politics* 39 (August 1977): 145–50.

———. *President Eisenhower and Strategy Management.* Lexington, Ky.: University Press of Kentucky, 1977.

Kissinger, Henry A. *The Necessity for Choice.* New York: Harper and Bros., 1961.

———. *Nuclear Weapons and Foreign Policy.* Garden City, N.Y.: Doubleday, 1958.

Kolodziej, Edward. *The Uncommon Defense and Congress, 1945–1963.* Columbus, Ohio: Ohio State University Press, 1966.

LaFeber, Walter. *America, Russia, and the Cold War, 1945–1975.* New York: Wiley, 1976.

Larson, Arthur. *Eisenhower: The President Nobody Knew.* New York: Charles Scribner's Sons, 1968.

Lilienthal, David E. *The Journals of David E. Lilienthal.* Vol. 3. New York: Harper and Row, 1966.

Lyon, Peter. *Eisenhower: Portrait of the Hero.* Boston: Little, Brown, 1974.

McLellan, David S. *Dean Acheson: The State Department Years.* New York: Dodd, Mead, 1976.

Major, John. *The Oppenheimer Hearings.* New York: Stein and Day, 1971.

Miller, Merle. *Plain Speaking: An Oral Biography of Harry S. Truman.* New York: Berkley, 1974.

Millis, Walter, ed. *The Forrestal Diaries.* New York: Viking, 1951.

———, Mansfield, Harvey, and Stein, Harold. *Arms and the State.* New York: Twentieth Century Fund, 1958.

Mills, C. Wright. *The Power Elite.* New York: Oxford University Press, 1956.

Mrozek, Donald J. "A New Look at 'Balanced Forces': Defense Continuities from Truman to Eisenhower." *Military Affairs* 38 (December 1974): 145–50.

Murphy, Charles J. V. "America's Widening Military Margin." *Fortune,* August 1957, p. 94.

———. "Anxious Aircraft 'Primes.'" *Fortune,* September 1957, p. 148.

———. "The Budget—and Eisenhower." *Fortune,* July 1957, p. 96.

———. "Defense: The Revolution Gets Revolutionary." *Fortune,* May 1956, p. 100.

———. "The Eisenhower Shift." *Fortune,* January, February, March, and April 1956.

————. "Eisenhower's Most Critical Defense Budget." *Fortune,* December 1956, p. 112.

————. "Eisenhower's White House." *Fortune,* July 1953, p. 75.

————. "Is the H-Bomb Enough?" *Fortune,* June 1954, p. 102.

————. "New Air Situation." *Fortune,* September 1955, p. 86.

Nelson, Donald. *Arsenal of Democracy.* New York: Harcourt, Brace, 1956.

Nixon, Richard M. *Six Crises.* Garden City, N.Y.: Doubleday, 1962.

Norton-Taylor, Duncan. "The Wilson Pentagon." *Fortune,* December 1954, p. 98.

Parmet, Herbert S. *Eisenhower and the American Crusades.* New York: Macmillan, 1972.

Patterson, James T. *Mr. Republican: A Biography of Robert A. Taft.* Boston: Houghton, Mifflin, 1972.

Phillips, Cabell. *The Truman Presidency.* New York: Macmillan, 1966.

Polenberg, Richard M. *War and Society.* Philadelphia: Lippincott, 1972.

Proxmire, William. *Report from Wasteland.* New York: Praeger, 1969.

Pusey, Merlo. *Eisenhower the President.* New York: Macmillan, 1956.

Rather, Dan, and Gates, Gary Paul. *The Palace Guard.* New York: Harper and Row, 1974.

Reichard, Gary W. *The Reaffirmation of Republicanism: Eisenhower and the 83rd Congress.* Knoxville, Tenn.: University of Tennessee Press, 1975.

Ridgway, Matthew B. *Soldier.* New York: Harper and Bros., 1956.

Ries, John C. *The Management of Defense.* Baltimore, Md.: Johns Hopkins University Press, 1964.

Rogow, Arnold A. *James Forrestal: A Study in Personality, Politics, and Power.* New York: Macmillan, 1963.

Roherty, James M. *Decisions of Robert S. McNamara.* Coral Gables, Fla.: University of Miami Press, 1971.

Rovere, Richard. *Affairs of State: The Eisenhower Years, 1952–1956.* New York: Farrar, Strauss, and Cudahy, 1956.

————. "Eisenhower over the Shoulder." *American Scholar* 31 (Spring 1962): 176–79.

————. "Eisenhower Revisited: A Political Genius? A Brilliant Man?" *New York Times Magazine,* 7 February 1971, p. 14.

————. *Senator Joe McCarthy.* New York: Harcourt, Brace, 1959.

Schilling, Warner R., Hammond, Paul Y., and Snyder, Glenn H. *Strategy, Politics, and Defense Budgets.* New York: Columbia University Press, 1962.

Serrin, William T. *The Company and the Union.* New York: Alfred A. Knopf, 1973.

Shannon, William V. "Eisenhower as President: A Critical Appraisal of the Record." *Commentary* 25 (November 1958): 390–98.

Sloan, Alfred P. *My Years with General Motors.* Garden City, N.Y.: Doubleday, 1964.

Solberg, Carl. *Riding High: America in the Cold War.* New York: Mason and Lipscomb, 1973.

Stern, Philip M. *The Oppenheimer Case: Security on Trial.* New York: Harper and Row, 1969.

Strauss, Lewis. *Men and Decisions.* Garden City, N.Y.: Doubleday, 1962.

Taylor, Maxwell D. *Precarious Security.* New York: Norton, 1977.

———. *Swords and Plowshares.* New York: Norton, 1972.

———. *The Uncertain Trumpet.* New York: Harper and Bros., 1960.

Theoharis, Athan. *Seeds of Repression.* Chicago: Quadrangle, 1971.

Thomas, Lately. *When Even Angels Wept.* New York: William Morrow, 1973.

Tobin, James. "The Eisenhower Economy and National Security." *Yale Review* 47 (March 1958): 321–34.

Truman, Harry S. *Memoirs.* Vol. 2. Garden City, N.Y.: Doubleday, 1956.

Truman, Margaret. *Harry S. Truman.* New York: William Morrow, 1973.

Tuchman, Barbara W. *Stilwell and the American Experience in China, 1911–1945.* New York: Macmillan, 1971.

Twining, Nathan F. *Neither Liberty nor Safety.* New York: Holt, Rinehart, Winston, 1966.

U.S. Congress. House. Committee on Appropriations. *Department of Defense Appropriations, 1954. Hearings before a Subcommittee of the Committee on Appropriations.* 83d Cong., 1st sess., 1953.

———. *Department of Defense Appropriations, 1955. Hearings before a Subcommittee of the Committee on Appropriations.* 83d Cong., 2d sess., 1954.

———. *Department of Defense Appropriations, 1956. Hearings before a Subcommittee of the Committee on Appropriations.* 84th Cong., 1st sess., 1955.

———. *Department of Defense Appropriations, 1957. Hearings before a Subcommittee of the Committee on Appropriations.* 84th Cong., 2d sess., 1956.

———. Committee on Armed Services. *Department of Defense Personnel. Hearings before a Subcommittee of the Committee on Armed Services.* 83d Cong., 2d sess., 1954.

————. *National Defense Policy. Hearings before the Committee on Armed Services.* 84th Cong., 1st sess., 1955.

————. *National Reserve Plan. Hearings before a Subcommittee of the Committee on Armed Services.* 84th Cong., 1st sess., 1955.

————. Senate. Committee on Appropriations. *Department of Defense Appropriations, 1954. Hearings before a Subcommittee of the Committee on Appropriations.* 83d Cong., 1st sess., 1953.

————. *Department of Defense Appropriations, 1955. Hearings before the Subcommittee of the Committee on Appropriations.* 83d Cong., 2d sess., 1954.

————. *Department of Defense Appropriations, 1957. Hearings before a Subcommittee of the Committee on Appropriations.* 84th Cong., 2d sess., 1956.

————. Committee on Armed Services. *Airpower. Hearings before a Subcommittee of the Committee on Armed Services.* 84th Cong., 2d sess., 1956.

————. *Ammunition Supplies in the Far East. Hearings before the Committee on Armed Services.* 83d Cong., 1st sess., 1953.

————. *Department of Defense Nominations. Hearings before the Committee on Armed Services.* 83d Cong., 1st sess., 1953.

————. *Doctor Draft Act. Hearings before the Committee on Armed Services.* 83d Cong., 2d sess., 1954.

————. *National Reserve Plan. Hearings before the Committee on Armed Services.* 84th Cong., 1st sess., 1955.

Wellman, Paul I. *Stuart Symington: Man with a Mission.* Garden City, N.Y.: Doubleday, 1960.

Wilson, Charles E. "Don't Underestimate American Strength." *Nation's Business* 43 (January 1955): 32–33.

————. "More Defense for Every Dollar." *Nation's Business* 44 (January 1956): 30–31.

————. "We Are Changing Our Strategy." *Nation's Business* 42 (January 1954): 34–35.

Wilson, Rose Page. *General Marshall Remembered.* Englewood Cliffs, N.J.: Prentice-Hall, 1968.

Wise, David, and Ross, Thomas. *The U-2 Affair.* New York: Random House, 1962.

Index

Acheson, Dean, 30–32, 65, 192n2
Adams, Sherman, 91, 157
Aiken, George, 154
Air Force, 23, 27, 29–30, 52, 70, 92, 101, 104, 109, 114, 125–26, 167–68, 182, 196n1, 197n26; controversy over preparedness, 132–48; opposition to reduced defense expenditures, 71–78
Alsop, Joseph, 68
Alsop, Stewart, 68
American Labor party, 89, 93, 192n20
Anderson, Frank C., 55
Anderson, Robert B., 25, 52, 114
Appropriations Committee (House of Representatives), 69, 70–71, 106, 114, 132–33, 197n14
Appropriations Committee (Senate), 74–76, 106–7, 114, 133, 175, 180, 198n36
Armed Services Committee (House of Representatives), 30, 132, 151, 160–61
Armed Services Committee (Senate), 21, 61–62, 74, 111, 126, 132, 151, 198n40; hearings on amendments to Doctor Draft Act of 1950, 93–95; hearings on Wilson's nomination as secretary of defense, 40–54
Army, 23, 27–29, 36, 52, 70, 74, 89, 101, 104, 107, 108, 109, 114, 126, 151, 160, 161, 167–68, 181, 182, 190n14, 192n20, 195n22, 196n1, 197n26; opposition to New Look, 118, 121–24, 132–38
Army-McCarthy Hearings, 86, 92–98

Assistant secretaries of defense, 23, 63, 64–65, 166–67, 190n11
Atomic Energy Commission, 86–88, 192n14

Baldwin, Hanson, 59, 63, 161
Benson, Ezra Taft, 187n3
B-52, 115, 126, 139, 140
Board of Review of Discharges, 95
Board of Review of Military Records, 95
Borden, William L., 86–87
Bradley, Omar N., 35, 61, 62, 64, 65
Bray, William, 152
Bridges, Styles, 46, 140
Brooks, Jack, 152
Brown, Harold, 182
Brownell, Herbert, 41, 87, 187n3
Brucker, Wilber, 161
Brundage, Percival, 174, 175
Bush, Vannevar, 62
Byrd, Harry F., 50, 61, 109

Carney, Robert, 67
Carroll, Wallace, 136–37
Casberg, Melvin, 190n11
Case, Francis, 158
Central Intelligence Agency, 22, 83, 195n25
Chamber of Commerce (United States), 85, 98
Chavez, Dennis, 115–16, 141, 152, 158
Chevalier, Haakon, 87
Chiang K'ai Shek, 31, 66
Chrysler Corporation, 50

Clark, Mark, 35, 61
Clay, Lucius, 42, 48
Clifford, Clark, 182
Cohn, Roy, 95, 193n26
Collins, J. Lawton, 61, 64
Colmer, William, 47, 48, 188n14
Cooper, John Sherman, 51, 93
Corrdry, Charles, 140
Council on Foreign Relations, 105
Cutler, Robert, 87

Dale, Ernest, 157
Davies, John Paton, 84
Defense Supply Management Agency, 63
Department of Defense, 13, 19, 20,
    42–45, 48, 59, 60, 62–63, 65–67, 71, 73,
    80, 82, 84–85, 93–94, 96–97, 98–99,
    114, 115, 130, 142, 151, 152, 156,
    161–62, 178, 179, 184n16, 187n4; his-
    tory of, 1947–52, 21–34, 202n11; Wil-
    son's approach to management of,
    38–39, 164–77
Department of State, 16, 28, 32–33, 82,
    84, 95, 98, 99
Dewey, Thomas, 27
Dirksen, Everett M., 91
Doctor Draft Act of 1950, 89, 92, 193n29;
    hearings on amendments to, 93–95
Dodge, Joseph, 69, 100–101, 174
Douglas, Paul, 52
Drucker, Peter F., 38
Duff, James, 198n42
Dulles, John Foster, 14, 178, 184n8,
    187n3, 194n7, 194n8; appointed sec-
    retary of state, 41; Cold War rhetoric
    of, 15, 18, 105; and loyalty procedures,
    84–85, 95, 96; in Korea with Eisenhower,
    65, 100; personal style of, 14; role in
    developing New Look, 104; speech to
    Council on Foreign Relations, 105
Durkin, Martin, 187n3

Eisenhower, Dwight D., 13–20, 35, 59, 72,
    74, 78, 81, 100–102, 110, 119, 121–22,
    136, 146, 151, 157–58, 170, 173–75,
    179, 182, 183n1, 184n8, 184n16,
    187n3, 187n4, 187n7, 194n6, 194n8,
    198n46; criticizes Wilson, 154–56; and
    defense reorganization, 64, 65; and
    Oppenheimer case, 86–89; prepresi-
    dential association with Wilson, 41–42;
    as presidential candidate, 17, 60, 102;
    problems with McCarthy, 83–84,
    89–92, 97–99; reputation as military
    expert, 18–19, 112, 117–18, 144; role in
    air power controversy, 133, 135, 142,
    144; role in developing New Look,
    102–20; role in Wilson's confirmation
    hearings, 41–42, 48–49, 54, 55, 57;
    views on defense administration and
    management, 17–18, 19, 37–38, 41, 164,
    168, 176–77; views on defense policy,
    180–81; views on economic policy,
    67–68; views on military opposition to
    administration policy, 124, 130, 133,
    142; works on passage of military bud-
    gets, 105–8, 112, 117
Eisenhower, John, 35
Eisenhower, Milton, 62
Ellender, Allen, 115
Ervin, Sam, 141, 143–44, 198n42
Evans, Ward, 88, 192n14

Ferguson, Homer, 61, 74, 107, 110,
    195n17
Flemming, Arthur, 62, 87
Floete, Franklin, 167, 190n11
Fohlen, Mrs. G., 158
Ford, Gerald R., 197n14
Ford Motor Company, 50
Forrestal, James V., 21, 37, 42, 182,
    185n2; as secretary of defense, 22–28,
    29, 33, 164–65; as secretary of the
    navy, 26
Fulbright, J. William, 152

Galusha, Mark, 151
Gardner, Trevor, 131, 133
Gates, Thomas, 170–71, 182
Gavin, James, 174, 180–81
General Motors Corporation, 14, 178,
    183n5, 188n13, 188n14, 188n15,
    188n21, 189n28, 189n33, 195n17; Wil-
    son's career at, 34, 36–37, 45; Wilson's
    experience at on administration of De-
    fense Department, 38, 64–65, 165–70,
    172–73, 176; Wilson's stock holdings in,
    40–41, 44–52
Goldwater, Barry, 151, 158
Gore, Albert, 109
Government Advisory Committee on
    Atomic Energy, 86
Government Operations Committee
    (House of Representatives), 64
Government Operations Committee
    (Senate), 89–90, 95–96, 99

Gray, Gordon, 87
Green, Roy, 160
Green, Theodore F., 151
Guerard, John W., 160

Hagerty, James, 49, 130
Handy, Thomas, 78
Hannah, John A., 190n11
Hayden, Carl, 78
Hendrickson, Robert, 46
Hensel, H. Struve, 65, 96, 98, 164, 190n12
Hoover, J. Edgar, 86, 96–97
Hughes, Emmett John, 83, 102, 149
Hull, John E., 171
Humphrey, George M., 15–16, 19, 41, 65–66, 74, 100–101, 104, 119, 173–74, 184n8, 187n3, 189n31, 194n6; and hearings on nomination as secretary of the treasury, 54–57; role in developing New Look, 104–5; views on defense spending, 16
Humphrey, Hubert H., 77–78, 108–9, 117, 181
Huntington, Samuel P., 23

Jackson, Henry, 114, 122, 126, 131, 181, 195n17; differences with Wilson, 141–44, 198n42
Jackson, Stephen, 161
Jameson, David K., 158
Johnson, Louis, 24, 26, 37, 45, 66, 165, 186n22; as secretary of defense, 28–32
Johnson, Lyndon B., 46–47, 54, 70, 74, 92, 108–9, 152, 180, 181
Johnson, Robert, 64
Johnston, Olin, 52
Joint Chiefs of Staff (JCS), 61, 76–77, 101, 112, 130, 133, 137–38, 165, 170, 173, 198n40; place in defense reorganization, 63–67; selection of new members of, 59, 64–67
Joint Congressional Committee on Atomic Energy, 86

Kefauver, Estes, 93–94, 130–31, 152, 180
Kennan, George F., 84
Kennedy, John F., 34, 108–9, 181
Kerr, Robert, 57
Khrushchev, Nikita S., 17
Kilgore, Harley, 52
Kindl, Carl, 162
Klein, Julius, 160

Knowland, William, 115, 117
Knudsen, William, 36, 45
Korean War, 16, 21, 31–34, 58–60, 68, 70, 80, 100, 101, 107, 121, 151–52, 162, 165, 172, 178, 179, 184n8; "shell shortage" alleged, 61–62; Truman administration's conduct of, 31–34; Wilson's concern with, 59–62, 80
Kyes, Roger, 25, 52, 165

Laird, Melvin, 182
Lamme, B. J., 36
Lawrence, David, 189n27
Lawrence, William A., 154
Lehman, Herbert, 52
LeMay, Curtis, 76, 138, 198n36
Leviero, Anthony, 137, 197n27
Lilienthal, David, 88
Long, Russell, 152
Lovett, Robert S., 24–26, 42, 62, 182; as secretary of defense, 32–34, 37

Maas, Melvin, 160
MacArthur, Douglas, 31–33, 197n27
McCarthy, Joseph R., 15, 29, 61, 81, 82–87, 89–92, 98–99, 110, 191n1, 192n2, 192n6, 192n20, 193n26. *See also* Army-McCarthy Hearings
McClellan, John, 61
McElroy, Neil, 182
McKay, Douglas, 187n3
McLeod, Scott, 84, 95, 96
McNamara, Patrick, 110
McNamara, Robert, 182
McNeil, Wilfred J., 164, 168, 190n11
M. A. Hanna and Company, 41, 55
Mansfield, Mike, 109
Martin, Edward, 151, 158
Marine Corps, 115, 117, 134, 160
Marshall, George C., 24, 26, 37, 42, 62, 82, 157, 182; as secretary of defense, 32–33
Maybank, Burnett, 78, 108
Mead, James, 47
Metheny, Lyal C., 136, 138
Miller, Merle, 83
Millikin, Eugene, 56
Missile systems, 174, 176
Monroney, Mike, 109
Moran, George, 152
Morgan, Thomas, 87
Morse, Wayne, 52, 76, 78, 152
Mundt, Karl, 96–97

Munitions Board, 63, 65
Murphree, E. V., 133

Nash, Frank, 190n11
National Guard, 64, 190n14; controversy
    over training requirements, 156–63,
    200n17
National Guard Association (NGA), 150,
    152, 157, 159
National Reserve Plan (NRP), 150–51
National Security Act of 1947, 22, 185n3;
    amendments to, 23; provisions of, 21;
    weaknesses of, 23, 26
National Security Council (NSC), 22, 170;
    NSC-68, 16, 31, 184n9; NSC 162/2, 102
National Security Resources Board, 22,
    59
Navy, 23, 27, 52, 70, 75, 92, 101, 104, 114,
    125–26, 132, 134, 167–68, 196n1; "Re-
    volt of the Admirals," 29–30, 66
Neely, Matthew, 52
Nelson, Roger, 193n29
Newberry, Frank, 190n11
New Look, 82, 99–100, 104, 119, 121–22,
    180; components of, 102, 105, 112,
    118; first budget, 1954, 106–10; second
    budget, 1955, 112–17; third budget,
    1956, 126–48
Nimitz, Chester, 62
Nixon, Richard M., 83–84, 192n6
North Atlantic Treaty Organization
    (NATO), 33

Office of the Secretary of Defense (OSD),
    24, 164, 167
Operation Clean Sweep, 166–67
Oppenheimer, J. Robert, 85–89, 192n14

Patterson, Robert, 26
Pentagon. *See* Department of Defense
Peress, Irving, 89–90, 93, 98, 192n20,
    193n29
Person, Wilton J. (Jerry), 91
Pike, Thomas, 190n11

Quarles, Donald, 190n11

Radford, Arthur, 78, 100, 115, 125, 130,
    173; role in developing New Look, 104;
    selected chairman of Joint Chiefs of
    Staff, 65–66
Reckord, Milton, 152
Remy Electric Company, 36
Reorganization Plan 6, 62–65, 166–67

Research and Development Board, 63
Reuther, Walter, 36, 195n17
Ridgway, Matthew, 33, 66, 78, 90, 117,
    133, 170; opposed to New Look, 118,
    124; publication of excerpts from *Sol-
    dier*, 126–31, 137, 196n3, 196n9,
    197n13, 197n14, 198n40
Rockefeller, Nelson, 190n10; and Reor-
    ganization Plan 6, 62–65, 167, 176
Roosevelt, Franklin D., 26, 29
Roosevelt, Theodore, 157
Root, Elihu, 157
Rumsfeld, Donald, 182
Russell, Richard, 46, 54, 110, 114, 122,
    131, 132, 181, 198n40; attacks Wilson,
    141; and conflict of interest issue, 51

Saltonstall, Leverett, 61, 110, 158; and air
    power hearings, 144, 198n42; and Wil-
    son's confirmation hearings, 45, 48–52
Sarnoff, David, 62
Schine, G. David, 92, 94, 99, 193n26
Schlesinger, Arthur M., Jr., 189n27
Schlesinger, James, 182
Scott, Robert, 196n26
Seaton, Fred, 172, 190n11
Shepley, James, 146
Sherwood, Robert, 185n2
Sloan, Alfred P., Jr., 36, 38, 165–66, 167,
    186n32, 187n2, 188n21
Smathers, George, 141
Smith, Margaret Chase, 94
Smith, Robert W., 201n27
Smith, Willis, 52
Soviet Union, 16–17, 27, 68, 74, 105–6,
    109–10, 126, 131–33, 134, 139, 142,
    175–77, 184n16, 194n8, 195n25,
    198n46
Stennis, John, 110, 115, 117
Stevens, Robert T., 25, 52, 78, 89–91,
    95–98, 161, 193n26
Stimson, Henry, 29, 157
Stone, Irving, 194n6
Stratton, William, 195n17
Strauss, Lewis, 87–88
Sullivan, John L., 30
Summerfield, Arthur, 187n3, 187n7
Symington, Stuart, 30, 45–46, 70, 93, 125,
    181; chairman of Senate Subcommittee
    on the Air Force, 132–33, 142–46,
    198n42, 198n46; criticizes defense pol-
    icy, 77, 108–9, 114–17, 122–23, 126,
    130–31, 195n24, 195n25, 197n13; as
    secretary of the air force, 30, 45, 125

Taft, Robert A., 32, 48, 83, 187n7;
criticizes Wilson, 42, 61; role in selection of Joint Chiefs of Staff, 59, 65–67
Talbott, Harold, 25, 52
Taylor, Maxwell D., 133, 158, 161, 170,
198n31; and interservice rivalry, 136,
138; selected Army chief of staff, 118,
124–25
Thomas, Charles, 165, 167
Truman, Harry S., 15–17, 22–34, 42, 45,
65, 72, 83, 87, 100, 181, 183n5, 184n17,
197n27; and NSC-68, 16–17, 31; as
senator, 47, 48; compared with Wilson,
15, 183n5
Truman, Margaret, 28
Twining, Nathan F., 67, 115, 133, 138

United Auto Workers (UAW), 36–37,
195n17
United Nations, 18

Vandenberg, Hoyt, 74–76, 80, 191n38
Van Fleet, James, 35, 61–62
Vietnam, 17–18, 181
Vincent, John Carter, 84
Vinson, Carl, 30
Voice of America, 83

Walsh, Ellard, 151, 152, 159–60, 201n27
Weeks, Sinclair, 187n3
Welch, Joseph, 95–96, 98
Westinghouse Corporation, 35–36
Westmoreland, William, 138
Williams, James T., 157
Wilson, Charles E.: administrative style
of, 19, 37–39, 164–77, 194n10, 202n13;
and air power controversy, 114–16,
131–35, 139–47, 198n28, 198n46;
analyzes problems of Defense Department, 68–69; business career of, 36–37,
186n32, 187n34; childhood and educa-
tion of, 35–36, 186n29; compared with
Truman, 15, 183n5; criticized by military leaders, 76, 126–31, 151–52, 174,
191n38, 196n3, 197n13, 198n31;
defends budget, 70–78; evaluation of as
secretary of defense, 178–82; hearings
on nomination as secretary of defense,
40–54, 187n2, 188n17, 189n27,
189n28; and National Guard controversy, 150–63, 200n13, 200n17,
201n27; relationship with General
Motors Corporation, 34–37, 40–52,
188n13, 188n14, 188n15, 189n24,
189n33; role in the New Look,
102–4, 105–18, 124–48, 194n6; selected
for cabinet, 21, 41–42, 187n3, 187n4;
testimony regarding Korean "shell
shortage," 61–62; views on defense
spending, 17–18, 194n6; views on
McCarthyism and internal security, 15,
91–92, 93–99, 192n8; views on
Vietnamese conflict, 1954, 17–18, 181
Wilson, Jessie (Mrs. Charles E.), 40, 156–
57, 162, 178
Wood, Leonard, 157
Woodring, Harry, 29
Wright, Jerauld, 78

Yeuell, Donovan, 136, 138
Yorty, Sam, 73–74, 191n35

Zwicker, Ralph, 89–90

E. Bruce Geelhoed was educated at Hope College (B.A., 1970), Central Michigan University (M.A., 1972), and Ball State University (Ph.D., 1975). He is currently director of the Carmichael Residential Instruction Project at Ball State University, where he also teaches courses in American history. He has previously taught in the Jenison, Michigan, public schools.

The manuscript was edited by Sherwyn T. Carr. The book was designed by Robert L. Nance. The typeface for the text and display is Baskerville, based on an original design by John Baskerville in the eighteenth century.

The text is printed on International Paper Company's Bookmark text paper, and the book is bound in Holliston Mills' Kingston Natural Finish cloth over binder's boards. Manufactured in the United States of America.